I Am Not Afraid of the Boogey Man

Darlene Wade

OVERCOMING THE SPIRIT OF FEAR

I Am Not Afraid of the Boogey Man
Overcoming the Spirit of Fear
by Darlene Wade

Printed in the United States of America

ISBN 9781609573225

www.xulonpress.com

DEDICATION

To the many people who encouraged me to follow this project
to the end—your love and support has been the wind beneath
my wings. God bless you.

To my children—you are the best thing that has ever happened to me, thank you for your time and energy invested in this
assignment.

To Harry D. Boomer and Dr. Bonnie C. Harvey—your unselfish
giving propelled me to fulfill a God given task. May the Lord God
continue to bless you abundantly.

To those who continue to fight the good fight of faith—don't
give up, don't back down and don't back out; God is able!

To the God of Abraham, Isaac and Jacob—Thank you.

CONTENTS

INTRODUCTION

There is no fear in love; but perfect love casteth out
Fear: because fear hath torment...
1 John 4:18

Problems from physical, mental, financial, geographical, hered-
itary, and the like have plagued individuals since the beginning of time. In my years of helping people solve their problems as a
friend, neighbor, relative, Pastor and a Social Worker, I have learned
a great deal about the obstacles people face on a regular basis.
Having said that, I believe many people I've talked to or counseled,
have as their biggest underlining problem that of fear. People have
shared some of their most intimate worries, anxieties and concerns
with me. These stories, along with my own, have caused an urgency
within me to want to do all I can to help the "fearfully bound" get
free.

It has humbled me as a helper and has taught me as a profes-
sional. My own life experience has shadowed much of what I've
heard. I have been a witness as well as an example as to how fear

can overwhelm an individual's life. Men, women, boys and girls have been haunted with experiences of fear that has robbed them of all courage and confidence. It has been a strong tormenting enemy; a force to be reckoned with. I can truly say that fear has torment and torture.

With all the chaos currently going on in the world; the wars, rumors of wars, earthquakes, hurricanes, murders, economy, etc., our society is growing more fearful. The catastrophic event of 9/11 has Americans more frightened than we've probably ever been. Economically, we are at an all-time low and hopelessness is running rampant in the land. No wonder a presidential candidate excited millions of individuals with words of hope, believe, we, us and change. These words speak life into what looks like hopeless situations.

We're afraid our past will catch up with us, afraid our future will not meet our needs let alone our wants, afraid we'll never be the person our heart longs to be, fear of failure; our goals won't be met, and fear that we'll die never having really lived. We're afraid to be alone, then we're afraid to be in a committed relationship. Many have sabotaged their own success for fear of being great and all that it entails; especially having it then somehow losing it. Fear has the capacity to render you useless to yourself and to others. The fear of today and the fear of tomorrow has become our guide; our leader. It has the ability to force one to live within the confinement of ones own mind. We make some of the most important decisions in our life based on fear. The proof is in the current condition of our government, our families, and our culture as a whole.

Fear is not prejudice against race, gender, political or economic status. Many people think it's for the poor, the underclass and the unsuccessful ones. However, it attacks world-renowned leaders, presidents, bishops, preachers, queens and kings. God forbid that fearful man may one day push the button that will set off the atomic bomb, killing us all.

The late Martin Luther King said it best when he stated, "In these days of catastrophic change and calamitous uncertainty, is there any man who does not experience the depression and bewilderment of crippling fear; which, like a nagging hound of hell, pursues our every footstep?" *(The Strength to Love)*

How long will we as individuals, as a nation, a world, allow fear to override the very essence of life? The greatness God has gifted us with must be utilized to the fullest. The life he has blessed us with must be lived to the utmost. It is time for us to stand tall as individuals; let our light shine to the glory of God. Our voice only hushed when we have met our expected end, the one planned since the beginning of time by the creator of our souls. To do this we need to deal with the issues that hinder us. In dealing with it, we overcome it, in overcoming it, we become the master and cease to be mastered.

The question is how do I deal with it? You may be saying, "I've been abnormally afraid of something or another all my life. I've tried and tried, nothing seems to work, somebody please tell me how do I overcome this obnoxious spirit of fear? What do I do with this leech, crusher, and troubler of my soul; where shall I begin?" I can only answer that question with what I did: "Begin with the truth."

This book reveals how the spirit of fear hindered me for many years. It exposes the tactics of the enemy. It also speaks of the inner struggles I faced on a daily basis in getting free from its stronghold. I believe each individual deals with life first from within then from without. Someone wrote, "A great civilization is not conquered from without until it's destroyed from within." The spirit of fear destroys from within. It begins by gnawing at your mind with seeds of doubt, negativity and terrorist tactics. Understanding this problem is the first step in dealing with it.

I have attempted to go back to the beginning where I believe the spirit of fear started with me. The following pages depict the struggles I faced from early childhood and far into my adult life. I pray with sincerity that someone will read these pages and know, no matter how hard you have previously tried you can still conquer fear. You do not have to exist in a bubble of fright. Those hidden fears and the invisible chains that bind you can be broken by the power of God. I encourage you to come out, come out from wherever you are. You too can win the battle over this deadly enemy called fear.

CHAPTER 1

THE BOOGEY MAN

The enemy pursues me, he crushes me to the ground; he
makes me dwell in darkness like those long dead. So
my spirit grows faint within me; my heart within me
is dismayed. I remember the days of long ago; I
meditate on all your works and consider what your
hands have done. I spread out my hands to you;
my soul thirsts for you like a parched land.
Answer me quickly, O Lord; my spirit fails.
Do not hide your face from me or I will be
like those who go down to the pit. Let
the morning bring me word of your
unfailing love, for I have put my
trust in you. Show me the way I
should go for to you I lift my
soul. Rescue me from my
enemies, O Lord for I
hide myself
in you.

(PSALM 143: 3-9 NIV)

As far back as I can remember the agony of tormenting fear has haunted me. Part of its origin could be the result of nightmares. I recollect being a three-year-old child suffering the devastation of horrifying, ghastly dreams. To this day I can still play reruns of those terrifying childhood dreams in my mind; they're like old black and white movies that never die out. The picture is incredibly vivid; it looks like a 3D version of "Nightmare on Elm Street."

I am still able to recall the "Boogey Man" chasing me. When we were children we often talked about the Boogey Man getting us. I don't know where that term originated, but I do know if somebody began to talk about the Boogey Man, we knew it was bad. We'd threaten each other with it by saying, "You'd better stop or the Boogey Man's going to get you." We thought that somewhere lurking in the shadows was a creature whose name was the Boogey Man. He was an unseen, unknown but somehow intimidating force. If you weren't scared of anything else, you were afraid of him.

The Boogey Man in my dreams was a big, black, fat, hairy creature that ran after me with extraordinarily long arms that stretched forward, grabbing harshly for my poor little soul. His fingernails were long, black and jagged. As my little legs jumped and leaped I tried with everything in me to stay free. I was running as fast as I could in total darkness, going around and around in circles with no safe place in sight; no protection, no covering, nobody standing in the gap, no safe haven. I was afraid he'd take me in his hands and crush me like a beetle. I'd fall and stumble getting up while he aggressively groped and grabbed; almost catching me as every second went by. Compared to my tiny little frame he was 20 feet tall, with big teeth and wide bright eyes encircled in blackness. He hovered over me like the creature from the Black Lagoon as I ran and screamed from the depths of my soul, in what seemed to be all night long. I would awake with unbelievable gripping fear, shaking like a leaf; oftentimes, I would go throughout the day still fearing the creature in my dreams, afraid somehow he'd show up at any given moment. The intensity of the dreams was incredibly real. When I woke up my body would be tired as if I actually burst out of the realm of darkness. It was as if my soul had been taken up into the evilness of night, terrified, and then thrown back into the natural world. This, I believe, is when the seed of abnormal fear was planted in me. Before I had a chance to learn about myself, before I knew who I was as a living, thriving, valuable human being, I was stricken with fear. It was like being born with an incurable disease; it was always there.

To add to that horror, I wet the bed every night. I can't remember which came first the chicken or the egg. I don't know if I had nightmares because of the consequences of wetting the bed, or if I was already having nightmares and the bedwetting was an added atrocity. Nevertheless, it was all hell. The consequence of the bed-wetting was a bed whipping, and it, along with nightmares, created in me an indescribable fear. Many nights I would try to stay awake petrified of the black monster but even more terrified of what would happen in the morning if I wet that bed. I had what you would call in the mental health field a "dual diagnosis." I had two fears going on from one extreme to the other. From the black demon in my dreams to the angry father who I was so afraid to wake up to; could they possibly have been one and the same?

Night after night I dreaded the hand that would inevitably reach down into the sheets before the sun rose; testing to see if they were wet. That hand would press hard under the covers, quickly maneuvering its way past the top blanket, snatching back the bedspread, reaching its ultimate destination; the urine-soaked sheet. That hand had no love; it didn't want to find a dry sheet. It was not unusual for me to be yanked up out of a terrible nightmare with the feel of that very hand slinging me high into the air, while the other hand held a relentless belt that slapped and wailed up my backside with a vengeance. When it was done it threw me down hurling insults as I lay powerless to its merciless chastisement. This enemy was heartless, unreasoning, tormenting; a "Black Monster," it was a traumatic experience, one that would last well into my adult life.

The seed of fear was planted in my dreams then watered through the beatings from bed-wettings; the result was a child whose soul was stricken with fear. Oh, the trepidation and the tears. This was the beginning of years entrapped in the iron-clasped grip of an invisible enemy. This enemy would use anything and anybody to keep me "scared to death." It forced me into the hibernation of my mind where I lived for many years; refusing to come out. Many adults would say, "Oh she's so shy," they didn't know the severity of the fear I was experiencing down to the core of my very being, down to the marrow of my bones where the blood is manufactured. It would have been more appropriate and more truthful to say, "My God, what is wrong with this child, she appears to be scared to death, it looks like she's seen a ghost." I suffered the constant fear of gloom and doom, always expecting some type of madness to occur. It was Aristotle who stated, "Fear is pain arising from the anticipation of evil." Aristotle, how right you were.

For me, dealing with fear was like playing a game of "hide-and-go-seek." It's a children's game where one player allows the other children to hide and then tries to find them. Most of us at some time have played it or maybe I'm revealing my age. Because today's children are so involved with modern technology they spend more time in front of the computer playing digital games instead of playing outside. When I was younger we played more physical games. After eating and completing our chores we couldn't wait to run outside to engage in recreation. We played all kinds of games; hopscotch, rock, kickball, dodge ball, etc. I'm sure some of these games sound antiquated to today's youth. Some games we made up as we played while other games were handed down from our parents. Hide-and-go-seek was one of the handed down games. This is one of those games we'll probably play until the end of time.

In this day and age they have the benefit of enjoying technology; however, one of its weaknesses is they lack the benefit of outdoor exercise, and the benefit of playing with many other children learning to socialize. Perhaps this explains the current problem we're facing in America with childhood obesity and the increase in childhood violence. The lack of exercise and socialization has created a need for a change that'll bring our children back to health and back to learning how to socialize properly with other children.

To our advantage we played outdoors for hours. Hide-and-go-seek was one of the games we played consistently. In this game the person who did the seeking would close their eyes, usually putting their head up against a tree or something. We'd all scurry around looking for the best place to hide; we hid under the porch, behind trees, in the neighbor's bushes or in the back of somebody's car. We didn't care how dirty we got or how crazy the hiding place was. It wasn't unusual to find somebody in a garbage can; ugh, now that we are so educated on germs and bacteria that's probably not an option.

You were who we called "It" if you were chosen to find where everybody was hiding. If the person who was It couldn't find you, they'd shout out, "Come out come out wherever you are." This was a taunting way of saying I'm still looking for you and you will be found. Most of the time, the person hiding didn't come out until they felt safe enough to hit that tree. If you could hit the tree before the person looking for you found you, then you had won your part of the game and they were still It.

I stayed petrified; to afraid to come out for fear I'd be caught before I could hit the tree and win the game. The fear of life was so embedded in me, I wouldn't dare attempt to win a game I thought was impossible to do. I would hide frozen in my position, fear raging within me, afraid I'd get caught. It wasn't the normal fear a child should have while playing a simple game.

We do the same thing when we hide out in life because we're afraid. Fear will have you peeping around every corner, asking yourself, "Why come out when there's safety in hiding and I probably won't win anyway?" We feel as though nobody can get us and nothing can hurt us if we keep hiding. Yet, every now and then we peep out and see some great things going on, things we want to be a part of. Within ourselves we know we have the ability to contribute greatly with our gifts, talents, abilities, knowledge and creativity. The greatness that nobody knows about but us and God. In our minds we visualize moving out in the richness of who we are. However, the spirit of fear will only allow you to peep out, wishing but not moving. All the while our creativity lies dormant and our ability to excel gets squashed in the process. We are literally hiding from the Boogey Man of our souls.

Fear will keep you hiding until the game is over. There is no possible way you can participate due to fear's agonizing grip. Therefore, you don't win or lose and for this reason many of us remain stagnated. Hiding hinders you, prevents you from fully living and creates a false since of security. I learned to hide at a very early age. Hiding became a way of coping. I hid behind excuses, people, any and everything I could find regardless to whether it was good or bad. That was my safety, my way of keeping me out of the hands of that "thing" that wanted to crush me like a beetle. I hid in the crevasses of my soul. This is not of God. The only place he wants us to hide is in Him.

Can you imagine the number of people who are hiding from the fear that stalks them; are you one of them? It stalks like a sociopath bent on having you whether you want him or not. Its ways are manipulative and controlling. It wants to run you, lock, stock, and barrel. It's also a pathological liar; its lies are relentless and dangerous. Its ways are deceitful, underhanded, unscrupulous and dishonest. Its attack is subtle, like the venomous bite of the serpent in the Garden of Eden. No matter how hard you try to rid yourself of its grip, it continues to hunt you down with viciousness compared only to a terrorist unafraid to die. There are nights you go to bed believing this is the day you kicked it, finally freedom has come to loose the chains that bind you, only to wake up in the morning with its ugly head rearing up even before your feet hit the floor. As you hide, its taunting voice is never far away, it whispers, "Come out come out from wherever you are."

If you're going to hide, do it in a way that's pleasing to the Lord. During a time of darkness and distress, David asked the Lord to deliver him from his enemies and to hide him. He said, *"Deliver me, O Lord, from my enemies: I flee unto You to hide me"* (Psalm 143). God is our refuge, our strong tower and our hiding place. He is able to protect us, to keep us in the secret place of the Most High, abiding under His shadow. Any other way is deceptive.

I know of another individual who wet the bed and went through agonizing suffering as a result of how it was handled. She's a sweet, kind, articulate and very intelligent soul. She tells a story of how her mother made her drink her own urine for wetting the bed. It was a cruel case of negative reinforcement.

Ignorance will cause us to allow the enemy to use us in the destruction of people whom we profess to love, those we should be nurturing.

Although it's been many years since this happened, the very thought of her having to drink her own urine brings sadness to my heart. She must have been about seven or eight years old; possibly older. My heart continues to ache for her at the thought of the humiliation and devastation she endured because of it. To this day I believe she has not effectively dealt with the consequences of her abusive childhood. She appears to be fearful of being who God has created her to be. She has been incarcerated, on crack cocaine, an alcoholic, has low self esteem, is eating herself into obesity and drinking herself into misery. She has hidden herself away in so many ways; in the bottle, men, drugs, deception, sex, food; whatever takes away the pain; even though it only brings temporary relief. She's afraid to come out and face the issues that hinder her; afraid to stand up and be counted as somebody. She's close to sixty years old and still running from the Boogey Man of her soul, peeping out every now and then only to retreat in fear. What more do you expect from a child who was terrorized during her developmental stages?

That's the bad news, but the good news is this: we can be healed and live positive, hopeful lives. One thing I have learned, when you call upon the name of the Lord, He hears, and He does answer. Your enemy has no power over God. When you put your faith in Him, fear only Him and believe in Him, He will show up. When He shows up, everything that's not like Him has to go. James said, *"Submit yourself to God resist the devil and he must flee"* (James 4:7).

My prayer for those of you who are suffering with the spirit of fear is that by the grace of God you experience total healing: body, soul and spirit. I pray that you become whole and fulfill the purpose and the plan God has designed for your life. That you come out from wherever you are, unafraid, and be all God has called you to be; all He has created you to be. I pray that you forgive if you haven't already, and run from your past into your destiny. That is my prayer for every person running from the Boogey Man.

Even now I shiver when I hear of parents whipping their child for wetting the bed. I'm not saying every child who's been spanked for wetting the bed is a case for the fear factor. I'm saying this particular way of dealing with this issue has the propensity to cause a child serious problems, one of them being the devastation of fear. Many children were spanked for wetting the bed and grew up to be just fine. Unfortunately, that is not the case with hundreds of others. It becomes a door for the enemy to come in, torment the child, and leave them with fear they are not capable of managing. Also, it depends on what spirit is operating behind the punishment.

A few years ago a young lady from a church I was attending called and informed me she was getting ready to "tear her son's behind up" for wetting the bed the previous night. In other words she was getting ready to "scare him straight" by beating his gluteus maximus to shreds. She said it with such authority that I knew she was dead serious and this poor child was in trouble. When she talked it sounded like her teeth were clinched, her words were angry; she was irritated. I'm so thankful she confided in me about the situation. I was able to immediately educate her on the misconceptions about bed-wetting. I reminded her that so far beatings had not cured the problem, and asked her to see a physician concerning this dilemma they were facing, before she "tore him up" again. I gave her my testimony on how I suffered as a child bed-wetter. She took my advice and as far as I know from that day forward he was no longer "torn up" for wetting the bed. Like my parents, and their parents, she was not knowledgeable on how to handle this particular problem. Regrettably, we're still perishing for lack of knowledge in areas we should be much more aware of. By her obtaining an understanding regarding her son's condition, he was saved from possibly being tormented for years.

Unfortunately, it is not uncommon for some adults to partake in the destruction of their own children, using this tactic as a means to cure their "bed wetting behavior" as well as other behaviors they feel are embarrassing or upsetting to them. We were whipped into shape; shamed; ridiculed; brought down to our knees in debilitating fear. It's a primitive form of teaching a child how to "behave." I pray that those who are still practicing this technique would stop immediately. IT DOES NOT WORK! I am a living witness and a perfect example that it is futile to continue this practice. Know this, if you spank a child day after day, year after year and they continue to wet the bed, you need to take them to see a doctor immediately; something is seriously wrong and you are contributing to the problem and not the solution. Furthermore, if you continue to spank a child for other negative behaviors you would like to see dispelled and the behavior continues; something is wrong, please seek help.

Sadly, for me this went on for almost the entire first seven years of my life. I grew up afraid of the dark, afraid of my father, afraid of doing something wrong, afraid of not being perfect, afraid, afraid,

afraid. The spirit of fear was working on me; it was in me, taking me on the rollercoaster ride from pure hell. The only power I had was in my mind. I could choose to be quiet; I could choose to shut the world out, I could choose to think how I wanted to think without interference. Therefore, I learned to be invisible, hoping and wishing that this would be a place of safety and that somehow all of this would go away.

Instead, it was a prison; a place where the spirit of fear had me in ball and chains. The "Boogey Man" was the boss. I could think whatever I wanted but I was afraid to share it. I could be quiet but it hindered the things I wanted to do and say. The development of my gifts, talents and abilities were stifled, hidden and bound by an invisible enemy. I'm sure somebody reading this knows exactly what I'm talking about. One thing I've learned about the spirit of fear is that we all experience much of the same thing. After speaking with individual after individual the stories are too similar to be a coincidence.

In 2 Timothy 1:7 the Bible talks about a "spirit of fear." It says *"for God has not given us the spirit of fear."* I believe he's referring to a disposition of the mind, a way of thinking. In Dr. Caroline Leaf's book *Who Switched off My Brain* she states "Fear is the root of stress. Fear is also a very real spiritual force. When fear enters the mind as a thought, you experience physiological changes that occur all the way down to the cellular level. This allows stress to cause negative and damaging alterations in your cells." (Pg. 53)

I wholeheartedly agree with Dr. Leaf. Fear is a very real spiritual force. It can cause extreme physical and spiritual damage to the human mind. I question whether children who have experienced a barrage of unnatural fear from a very early age are prone to sicknesses, diseases or psychosocial problems that they otherwise would not have. Dr. Leaf states, "Excessive levels of stress and the toxic thoughts and emotions it causes in children result in a greater susceptibility to illness and disease in body, mind and spirit. What parent would ever want that to happen to their child! As a parent you need to know that negative, fearful thoughts actually change your children's brain chemistry." (Pg. 87) In this book she does a wonderful job of exposing the results of toxic thoughts and emotions.

Negative conditioning is a friend to the spirit of fear. Let's call it a Lieutenant in fear's strategic army bent on destroying our very being. The search for who we are will be an unsuccessful journey when fear is allowed to lead the expedition. It will have you to believe your present condition is as far as you'll go. It may seem impossible to act in any way courageous when you're faced with unbearable fears. However, this is far from the truth. Our minds are capable of going places far above our current situations. For instance, a client I had as a social worker was a man about seventy-five years old, stated that when he was younger he thought he was the biggest coward in the world. He was afraid of speaking up to anybody for fear he would sound stupid and be laughed at. As a child his father called him stupid so many times that one day he simply accepted the fact that he was stupid. He had a fear that people would somehow find out how stupid he was. He would be in groups of people who were holding political, financial and spiritual conversations, he'd have great insight into what they were discussing, yet they would never know it. Every time he got ready to interject his own opinion, the spirit of fear would shut him down. It would interject fearful thoughts such as "You better not open your mouth; they'll laugh at your stupid remark." It shut him up every time. He said one day he got so tired of being the way he was that he began to act as though he was somebody else; the person he wanted to be. In other words he began to do it unafraid. This "somebody else" began to speak up and say things totally out of character from the man's fearful self. He said he felt so good doing it that he never went back to himself again. He thinks it's the most hilarious thing; you should hear him laugh when he talks about it.

Actually, what happened to him was he began to think higher of himself. Although he created an alter ego, he reached down into the part of him that was already there. It was simply hidden away, afraid. He wouldn't have been able to pull out anything, if in fact it didn't exist within. He basically found a way to deal with his fears. His mind took him places he previously feared to go.

The reality is we all have within us the power to succeed at being us. When we are engrossed in fear and self doubt it's hard to accept this. Nevertheless, just because you don't believe it doesn't mean it isn't so. When we began to think we can, then more than likely we will. If we believe we can't, then more than likely we won't. It has been a long journey for me and probably you too. Let us refuse to allow fear to be the author of our destiny.

If it had not been for the Lord who was on my side, eventually, I would have lost heart. Can it be that God gets an abundance of glory when a frightened child grows up to one-day stand unafraid and strong in Him? Thank God He's able to turn any situation around. All things do work together for good to them who love God, to them who are the called according to His purpose. God is able!

Anything that has bound you historically does not mean it will always have a grip on you. Trust in God He's able to set you free. You don't have to be afraid of the terror by night nor the forces of hell that come against you in the day. The Boogey Man is a liar! Our God is able to deliver us. He did it for me; He'll do it for you.

Let's Pray: Father, I thank you for being my hiding place. Oh Lord there are times when my spirit fails, but glory be to you whose unfailing love is a comfort unto me. I'm grateful for your love, your mercy, and your grace. Lord, where there is fear, give me courage. I trust and believe you are able to deliver me from this debilitating spirit. Amen.

1. Do you believe there is a spirit of fear?

_____

_____

2. Have you been hindered by this spirit?

_____

_____

3. Have you been through a traumatic experience you felt brought on the spirit of fear?

_____

_____

4. If you believe there is a spirit of fear, how will you begin to deal with it?

_____

_____

CHAPTER 2

SCARED STRAIGHT

So, first of all, let me assert my firm
belief that the only thing we have to
fear is fear itself — nameless,
unreasoning, unjustified terror
which paralyzes needed
efforts to convert
retreat into
advance.

— FDR - First Inaugural Address, March 4, 1933

Have you ever been attacked so bad by the spirit of fear that it affected you physically and mentally? There have been instances of people actually scared to the degree of going into shock, or even having heart attacks leading to death. Fear has the capacity to do that to you.

My sister and I were once on a ride at Euclid Beach, an old amusement park in Cleveland, Ohio. The ride was called the Hammer. I was about ten years old and she was about twelve. That ride scared the living daylights out of both of us. I knew before I got on the Hammer it was too much for me, I was a total scaredy cat anyhow. Even so, I thought it would be ok because she was on it with me. I never thought for one moment she'd be as scared as I was. You think everybody else is brave and you're the scared one? Think again, people are frightened by some of the same things that frighten you, they simply have a different way of showing it or should I say hiding it.

This ride had two big ends and was shaped to look like a hammer. We climbed in one of the ends, sat down and were strapped in. My heart was pounding so hard it probably looked like one of those cartoons where you see the heart pumping in and out of the body while the character grabs the wall and gasps for air. Before we knew it the ride went straight up several feet into the air then it dropped, fast and furious, swinging us around just to fly us back up into the air again for another drop. The idea was to appear as though a hand was holding it and using it as a hammer, pounding down on the ground forcefully. When it reached its height we would be upside down for a second or so. That second was like a lifetime. Then it would come down as if it were going to hammer something in the ground. I recollect us being so scared that we began to yell at the top of our lungs. She was crying, "stop, stop" and I was crying, "Mama, Mama help." My heart was pounding so hard I thought I was going to collapse and she looked as scared as I did. Tears were flowing down our faces like a river; I think we were yelling so loud they could hear us all over the park at least a mile away. It was a cry of pure agony. Our screaming was so wild that the attendant suddenly stopped the ride and allowed us to get off. He was loosing the seatbelt as fast as he could. He hastily ushered us off. People were standing around watching us as we hurried off, still crying, looking like we were petrified. We walked off like two little embarrassed, scared rabbits, vowing never in life to do that again.

When I look at the rides people get on today, I'm flabbergasted by their courage. If we yelled on that little Hammer, we would probably have a nervous breakdown on the stupendous rides that entertain today's thrill seeker. It scared me straight into never wanting to ride again. Over the years I continued to frequent amusement parks; however, I have never ever willingly placed myself on a ride like that one. My motto is "I don't trust man's ability to create something like that that'll keep me safe," and I let it be known, "I'm scared." Being afraid does not amuse me the least bit. Don't get me wrong, I'm not a total scaredy cat anymore. Having fun at an amusement park is something most people enjoy. I enjoy the games, the entertainment, the food and some of the rides; although I'm prejudicially selective. What I don't enjoy is seeing anyone scared straight out of their wits, and causing harm to their psyche. Plus, lately far too many rides have accidentally killed people, young and old.

The psychological and physical discipline countless children go through dealing with bed-wetting as well as other problematic behaviors can be like a program similar to "Scared Straight." This program is reportedly designed to help young people see where they will wind up if they don't straighten out their act. They are taken to a correctional facility and dealt a blow that is supposed to scare them straight. Juvenile delinquents, who are going nowhere fast, are yelled at and humiliated by prisoners in a therapeutic attempt to help them see the error of their ways and to modify their behavior. Fear is utilized as a power tool to straighten them out. The juveniles make a trip behind bars where a multitude of furious, hard-boiled convicts vocally and emotionally attempt to scare them straight. The goal is to make them have a visual and inner awareness of the possibility that if they ever have to be incarcerated for any reason, their life in prison will be a living hell. This process is supposed to give them a choice to choose between "good" or "bad." It's my understanding that for some of the juveniles this works, but for others it doesn't. Either they were going to pass up the warning of a lifetime or adhere to it and be rehabilitated. According to some parents their children weren't scared straight they were *scarred* straight. It's one thing to scare somebody, but it's another thing to scar them. They believed it only created distrust, unnatural fears, as well as resentment toward the adults who were attempting to provide them with a therapeutic approach to changing their lives before they were too far gone.

Similarly, people have attempted to scare others straight by using some of the same tactics. In my case, unlike the juveniles who were supposedly able to choose between whether they were going to straighten up and fly right, or continue on a road of destruction, I was not allowed the privilege of choice. Given an alternative, there never would have been another bed wetting morning for me; my life of crime would have been over after the first punishment. One morning of yelling, screaming and scorn would have been more than enough. All you had to do was "evil eye" me and I melted into the ground. I would have kept the sheets clean, woke up in the middle of the night to relieve myself in a proper fashion and never ever committed that crime again. I wasn't scared straight I was scarred straight; period.

The problem was I wanted to be scared straight. If the spanking was giving me a choice to choose between being good or bad, I chose good. However, I kept wetting the bed, every morning I got whipped for it and every night I was dreadfully fearful of it. I spent years afraid to go to sleep, for fear I would not wake up in time to use the bathroom. I hated myself for being a bed wetter. My self-esteem was destroyed, annihilated, aborted by the enemy of my soul. Somebody needed to take me to Jesus and tell Him how they couldn't cast this thing out. They tried to beat it out, scare it out, humiliate it out and shout it out. Yet, it didn't budge.

It was not until the year 1999 that I realized, when I went to the restroom to urinate, I would unconsciously make sure I was awake by holding it in for a few seconds before releasing myself. I had a subconscious fear that somehow I was dreaming and would wet the bed. I would sit on the stool, look around, and feel my legs in one last attempt to make sure I wasn't sleeping. At this time I hadn't wet the bed in over 35 years. It was also about this same time that I began to understand why I never slept throughout the night peacefully. I would wake up at least every twenty minutes. I had become so accustomed to making sure I didn't urinate in my sleep. In my subconscious mind there was an underlying fear of wetting the bed and having to suffer the consequence behind it. Unfortunately, the fear I received as a child was still in some fashion or form controlling me.

Thank God for deliverance! God turned the darkness of my life into the brightest light. His word is awesome; it will set you free. I was reading it, believing it and writing it in my heart. Scripture such as Psalm 129:2, *"Many a time they have afflicted me from my youth: yet they have not prevailed against me"* helped me to stay focused on His mercy and grace. God would make it personal and speak to my soul saying, *"Darlene, I know you were afflicted in your youth, yet, the enemy has not prevailed against you. I saw it all, I was with you every step of the way, I am righteous and I have cut asunder the cords of the wicked and because you dwell in the secret place of the Most High no harm shall come near you, no evil shall befall you, and no plague shall come near your house. Just rest in me, my child, for I am all you need."*

When He speaks to me like that I can feel the presence of Jehovah Shalom, my God of Peace. The Holy Spirit was doing a work in me and I am ever so grateful. He was and still is teaching me, leading me and guiding me into all truth. He is not a respecter of persons; He'll do it for you too. I was slowly but surely coming out from the place of fear that had hindered me for so long. I am a living witness that it can be done; come out from among the spirit of fear.

I don't know what has caused you to be locked up in fear. For many people it is some type of childhood traumatic experience a case of neglectful or abusive parents, absent parents, horrid foster care situations, bullies, as well as many other circumstances. There has been instances of accidents, such as plane and car crashes that have caused unexpected fear to begin controlling individuals. Young girls look at TV and fear not being able to meet the standard of perfection they witness on a daily basis. They fear getting fat so they starve themselves, they fear not being popular so they do immoral things to acquire acceptance within the "in crowd."

Sometimes we don't know where it came from. All we know is here it is and we need to get out of it and get out today. No matter the origin, there is a solution that will cause you to be released from its stronghold in your life.

First, you must trust in the Lord, knowing He is the God that made the Heavens and the Earth and if He made it He can surely help you and I in it. He is not a fictitious character from out of a comic book. Superman doesn't have anything on God. He doesn't have to leap tall mountains in a single bound to get to you. He simply removes them at His will, and He said you could do the same thing. All He asks is that you have faith the size of a mustard seed, then you'll be able to speak to the mountain and it will move from here to there. Life and death is in the power of the tongue. There is no secret about it. It's in the Word and always has been. It doesn't matter what kind of mountain it is, be it a mountain of fear, hate, addiction, debt; it can be cast into the sea, gone forever. What a mighty God we serve! Taste Him, try Him and see that He is "Oh, so good." Don't wait on fear to scare you straight, take on the spirit of power, love and a sound mind from the true and living God. He doesn't want to scare you straight. He wants to love you straight into His arms where you are safe. *"The name of Lord is a strong tower; the righteous man runs into it and is safe."* (Proverbs 18:10 ESV)

Second, you need to begin to change your thinking process. Allow the power of positive thinking to change the way you see things.

Fear depends on your participation to operate. It has a tendency to attack your thought process. If you bite the bait it's feeding you, it'll have you on the tip of its reel flapping like a fish out of water trying to get free. The bait changes depending on what type of fear you're being lured into. For example, if it's fear of crowds you'll have to bite the lie that crowds will somehow hurt you, hinder you, or the people are watching you. If it's fear of germs, you'll have to bite the lie that everything you touch could possibly cause a serious illness. If it's the fear of relationships, you'll have to bite the lie that everybody has an ulterior motive regarding you, and that because somebody once did you wrong everybody will. It'll try to bait you with every imaginable lie it can come up with.

Often times we've taken a bite of the enemies bait and not even realized it. It will creep up on you at the most inopportune time. It will pick your most vulnerable moment and plant seeds of doubt and fear. Times when you are at your weakest such as: times of death, during illness, as a young defenseless child, while separated from the ones we love, in times of war, in economic hardship, as well as many other times of vulnerability. We need something to make us feel better so we take a bite. Fear comes in and begins to work. Its main objective is to scare the living daylight out of you, leaving you in total darkness. Its desire is to control you with fearful thoughts, creating phobias, anxieties and depression. Thus it prevents you from fulfilling God's purpose and plan for your life.

I'm not talking about the fear of God, or fear that warns us of a potentially unpleasant situation, or circumstance such as sticking your hand in the fire. These are good fears. It's wonderful to receive warnings in relation to possible danger; without it, there would be total chaos in the land. I thank God that in His awesomeness He has created us with the ability to discern danger before it occurs. Even the ability to be fearful is a gift when placed in its proper perspective.

Fear has its place within us and within our society. It's a blessing that the fear of pain caused someone to invent anesthesia for surgery. The fear of spending hours upon hours riding on a horse in sub zero weather caused somebody to invent the automobile; with heaters. The fear of AIDS will cause a person to abstain from promiscuity, the fear of being penniless will lead a person to handle their finances responsibly and the fear of being sick will make a person take care of their health. We need these fears to assist us in making the right choices and decisions.

The most important fear to have is the fear of the Lord. It causes us to have a reverence for an almighty God, an awe of who He is. It's the guard on your heart that keeps you in check. Fearing Him causes us to abstain from sin and make the right choices. Sometimes his Spirit comes and causes us to have a healthy fear of him that dispels whatever's not like Him.

"Now all the people witnessed the thunderings, the lightning flashes, the sound of the trumpet, and the mountain smoking; and when the people saw it, they trembled and stood afar off. And they said unto Moses, You speak with us, and we will hear: but let not God speak with us, lest we die. And Moses said unto the people, Fear not: for God is come to prove you, and that His fear may be before your faces, that you sin not." (Exodus 20:18-20 NKJV)

There are times when I hear thunder and lightning and have a healthy fear of it. I visualize the creator of the universe having His way with the winds and the waves, being that they do obey Him. I can hear the Spirit of God saying, "Don't mess with me down there and don't forget I'm in control up here."

I've trembled in my boots many times saying, "Lord, I hear you. You don't have to do anything different to let me know you are God, there is none like you and you are the captain of this whole entire ship." Then I throw in there, "Please forgive me for trying to steer things my way, here take the helm, steer us where you want to go, I'll just get my little shipmate self here in the background and you tell me exactly what it is you would have me to do, because you are the boss." I'm grateful for this kind of fear, it keeps me in line with the Holy Spirit.

The fear we've got to beware of is fear coming from the Greek word *phobeo*, from which we get the word "phobia." This is an intimidating fear, a dreadful, frightening, destroying fear, leaving us confused and perplexed. Fear is one of the most toxic emotions when not put into its right perspective. So many things God has gifted us with to survive has been twisted, this is one of them.

It is not the desire of an all-powerful, all-loving God that man be fearful in a warped way. God doesn't want us so afraid that we allow fear to block faith. It is not pleasing to the Lord to see us acting and reacting out of fear. It's impossible to please Him without faith in who He is and what He says. He was warning us when He said He's not given us the spirit of fear but of power, love and a sound mind. The spirit of fear He's talking about here paralyzes you, makes you feel like you're stuck in time, stagnated, unable to go forward or backward. It's a fear that dominates your every thought, guides your every move, and can even pull you away from the very God of Gods whom you have professed out of your own mouth to be mighty, unbeatable, unsearchable and unshakable. It's a destroying, demon spirit; keep in mind it's a "spirit of fear."

This fear will make an individual abnormally fear that everyone around them probably has a contagious disease, so they avoid people like the plague, biting that bait. They isolate themselves from the very people God would use to bless them, people who will love them. It'll make an immensely wealthy individual so scared one day they'll be broke, that they choose to live on dog food rather than buy groceries because it's cheaper. These are some of the people that died and had thousands of dollars under the mattress. People called them cheapskates and misers but actually they were simply afraid. It'll make a person so afraid of getting sick from germs that they become a compulsive hand washer and stay away from everything and everybody, remaining isolated for fear of "contracting a nasty deadly disease." The fear is so powerful they wash their skin off, see the blood, and continue washing in spite of the damage it's causing them. Once this spirit has isolated them it begins to feed them additional words of fear and doubt. This fear is devastating; it wants to kill, steal and destroy. God is saying I have not given you that, and don't you accept it. He's saying the spirit I have given you will equip you with first, power, then love and a sound mind. He said it in His Word, believe it in your heart. You will see the fruition of it.

You may be saying to yourself, well, that's to the extreme I'm not afraid like that. Yet, God has given you the ability to sing like an angel and bless the nations but fear has its hand on your vocal cords. So you sit in the midst of the congregation with your mouth shut, silenced by a spirit with no true authority. God does not get any glory when His plan has been diverted. You may be a gifted architect but fear has kept you from creating beautiful edifices. You may be one of the most gifted writers who ever lived but fear and its capacity to destroy has told you there is no way you, of all people could ever write anything worth publishing; it has scared you straight into anonymity. The answer to the cure for cancer has probably already been revealed to one of God's chosen people. I pray the spirit of fear does not hinder them from coming forth. The fear of failure will prevent you from trying. I once heard that nothing beats a failure but a try. I have learned to believe it with all of my heart. There is a great need in the land for all God's people to position themselves, unafraid and unashamed to be exactly who He created us to be; fulfilling His perfect plan.

As a child one of my most fearful moments was in the midst of a storm; literally. At this time we lived in a small apartment with five children and two adults. I was only about three or four years old. I remember periods when the lights would go out due to thunderstorms. It would be unbearably noisy; you could hear every snap, crackle and pop as though it had its very own platform. The wind would be blowing hard, thunder roaring like the sound of an atomic bomb, while lightning wielded its electric force, all together they were fiercely out of control. For me it sounded like the end of the world. In a toddler's mind sounds are magnified. Probably like a dog I had named King. He was a golden retriever who hid under the bed every time it started thundering. As soon as he heard the first pop he looked up to the sky, ran for the bed and was scared straight under the mattress. He was so afraid of something he couldn't see or attack. Otherwise, when we let him out of the backdoor in the mornings, he ran out like the king of the jungle. He chased everything that moved out of the backyard. He killed skunks, rats, birds, and dared every squirrel perched on the telephone line to come down and deal with him. When he barked it sounded like a lion that roared just to let everything that moved in the backyard know I'm here and I'm bad. Yet, he was afraid of thunder; the sound of it was magnified in his mind. At first he used to bark at the sky but saw it wasn't getting him anywhere so he resorted to running. It was a major problem for him, partly because he couldn't see it; therefore, he couldn't attack it.

Likewise, this is how the spirit of fear often operates; you can hear the thunder, even see the lightning, but you can't see how to combat it. Like my dog, we run and hide. Afterwards, we come out, running off into the world ready to attack every situation until the sound of thunder roars again. I've seen people in the church shouting out, "I come against every foul filthy spirit and I command you to leave right now" and as soon as the spirit says "Boo" off they run. It scares them straight back into hibernating.

Back to the storms when I was a child. I remember one particular time when my father gathered us all in a circle and began to tell a story. He would tell scary stories and make creepy sounds. He'd talk about ghosts while distorting his face. He had big white eyes and he would bulge them out as far as they could go, all the while twisting his mouth and moving his ears. To this day, I don't know what is was about me, but I thought he would get pleasure out of singling me out and scaring me the most. Perhaps he got the biggest reaction out of me, the best laugh for himself or the sordid enjoyment to know his scaring tactics were highly effective. I can recall one particular incident quite clearly. He pulled my two sisters and two brothers close to him and left me sitting on the other side of the room; going out of my mind in fear. I trembled and shook; my little mind racing with uncontrollable fear. My brothers, sisters and I were back to back in age; one, two, three, four and five. I was the middle child. At this time the seed of fear was continuously being watered. I sat there hoping and wishing my mother would come through the door. I don't know why she wasn't there, perhaps she went to the store or something; I don't know. For the most part she was a stay at home mom and was always available. I only remember it was the most devastating time for me, I was horribly afraid.

I was a terrified child who grew up to be an extremely frightened adult. Fear stood in the way of virtually everything I ever wanted to accomplish. It was determined to keep me bound and I was hopeless and helpless in getting free. It was as though we had a slave-master relationship; it governed and I obeyed. Little did I know there was a spiritual connotation to all I was going through, even then. I was a child, with a child's mind, thrown into a world full of fear and despair; ill-equipped to fight the evil that lurked in the closet of my mind; waiting until I fell asleep to jump out and shout "Boo!" I was a little girl clueless to anything and anybody outside of my own world. I didn't realize that life didn't have to be the way I was experiencing it. I imagined this was the way it was supposed to be. I thought children got the hell beat out of them for wetting the bed. I thought fathers scared their children and other than whipping them had little else to say or do. As I grew older it was surprising to find out this was not true.

Because I've had to experience fear so much in my life I can see it, smell it, I know when it's operating in somebody. I see it in their faces, their actions and their reactions. It can't hide from me; I know it too well. It's not always in the one that looks scared, either. It's in the bully, the curser, the liar, the one who appears to be outgoing, the arrogant as well as in one who seems to be confident. That's why it's a spirit known to cause so much damage, it isn't always detectable. Unless you've been bound by it you may not be able to discern it. God will take the very thing you've suffered with, to help others who have suffered similarly.

It was surprising to find out many adults are not aware of the crippling result of fear. Countless individuals suffer due to the severity of fears ability to render them helpless. Fear has a hold on us like puppets on a string. We bounce around, up and down, to the left and to the right allowing fear to dictate what we say, do and feel. We're like the dummy while the spirit of fear is the ventriloquist. We say what it tells us to say having no mind of our own. One important thing to keep in mind is when you speak be aware of whether it's you or the spirit of fear. When we say things out of fear we are feeding into its grip. I must reiterate, life and death are in the power of the tongue.

Once again, the Word of God is warning us this type of fear is not from Him. This spirit has crippled many people. It has shattered countless dreams, destroyed lives, and prevented thousands upon thousands from being all they can be; all they were born to be; all they were created to be. I believe the enemy has "scared us straight" into believing everything he says and does to be the truth. When faced with fears, anxieties, worries and the like, we must remember one important thing; that we wrestle not against flesh and blood but against principalities, powers, rulers of the darkness of this world... (Ephesians 6).

We frequently question why children are subject to so much pain and sorrow. We pray to the Lord to keep our babies from hurt, harm and danger. It is inconceivable to think that the God of Gods we serve would allow a destructive devil anywhere near our babies. I believe God uses what the enemy meant for our destruction and turns it around for our good. He is sovereign. *"His dominion is an eternal dominion; His Kingdom endures from generation to generation. All the peoples of the earth are regarded as nothing. He does as He pleases with the powers of heaven and the peoples of the earth. No one can hold back His hand or say to Him: "What have you done?" (Dan. 4:34-35 NIV).*

I was reading the story of Jacob and Joseph one day when something struck me. I had always been under the impression that Joseph's brothers hated him because of the dream. However, in Genesis 37: 4 it states *"And when his brethren saw that their father loved him more than all his brethren, they hated him and could not speak peaceable unto him."* This taught me that they hated Joseph because the father loved him more. Then it dawned on me that the enemy of our souls hates us because the father loves us, not because of any dream we've had. Having dreams only makes him hate us more. The Word says, *"And Joseph dreamed a dream, and he told it his brethren: and they hated him yet the more"* (Gen: 37:5). In his dream his brothers would one day be bowing to him. They looked at him and said that'll be the day. They hated him for his dream and they hated him for talking about it.

I can picture his brothers wanting to scare him straight. They probably thought, "How dare him dream about us bowing down to him. Who does he think he is?" I can hear them saying, "We'll scare the hell out of him" and for the most part many of us would have been scared. Each one of us probably knows somebody, or maybe even our self, that has been scared out of their dreams.

Joseph could have been scared straight into believing his dream was a farce. But he didn't; he held onto the dream God gave him. Nowhere in the Bible does it say, "And Joseph was afraid so he gave up his dream."

They were so jealous that the spirit of hate and envy rose up in them to the point of having a murderous heart. They were afraid that somehow they didn't measure up to their father's love, and they were angry at the thought that he loved Joseph more. I believe the spirit of fear scared them straight into wanting to get rid of their problem. Thanks to their brother Reuben, they didn't kill him. But, they sold him to the Midianites merchantmen and the Ishmaelites who made a market out of him. In their feeble attempt to get rid of the problem they were in essence bringing to fruition the dream they so despised.

Then, in perfect harmony with that spirit's character, it had them to lie and tell Jacob his son had died. See, the spirit of fear will have you doing the stupidest things. First, it baits you and gets you all caught up in its trap. Then it watches as you wriggle around entrapped by a spirit that has no mercy.

I can imagine Jacob's hurt when he thought his precious son Joseph was dead. I can also imagine how it grieves the Spirit of God to see us operating out of a spirit of fear, sold out to a bill of lies with the intent to hinder us for as long as it can.

Joseph's brothers may have thought they sold him out but they sold him into his promise; because of God he went from the pit to the palace. In the end he told his brothers what you meant for bad God meant it for good, that much people might be saved. Joseph's trials and tribulations as a young man made him stronger as he got older. He is a perfect example as to how God can turn things around. His life is indicative as to how God can use the fear of others that rages in jealousy and envy to benefit you, and oftentimes, even them.

Don't think that because things have happened to you because of fear means you're sold out and it's over. It's possible that it is just beginning, like Joseph, that much people might be saved. When you come out of this trial you'll be stronger, wiser, full of the power of God, able to withstand the storms of life.

Haven't you heard children enthusiastically talk about what they're going to be when they grow up? They innocently express their dreams about becoming scientists, doctors, astronauts, athletes, soldiers, teachers, nurses and preachers.

I once heard an eight-year-old say he was going to find the cure for cancer. He said God gave it to him but he's got to get bigger so he can put it together. His mother looked at him, smiled and said, "He's been saying that since he was about three years old."

We need to be aware that just like Joseph revealed his dreams, enraging his brothers, something is listening when children reveal their dreams and aspirations. That something is the spirit of fear. It heard and is waiting for a chance to plant seeds of doubt and fear.

Apparently the enemy knows the anointing on our lives. He tries to destroy it before a foundation can be built. He has tried to kill babies since the beginning of time. He killed babies in an attempt to kill Moses and in an attempt to kill Jesus. His question is, "Who has the anointing and whose dream can I destroy?" His answer is find them and destroy; the sooner the better. He has no sense of conscience about children. Remember he's the same one who rebelled against God and took a third of the angels with him. If he can't kill you, he'll scare you to death. He'll put thoughts into your mind that will eventually make you want to give up.

The spirit of fear will cut a youngster down, fast, and in a hurry. Why? Because children are vulnerable to its tactics. Once they've had a chance to grow strong, it's not that easy. It's like pulling the roots up out of an oak tree before the trunk has had the opportunity to grow.

The oak tree can grow to be very big and strong. Its height can reach over a hundred feet tall. This tree has been known to be a symbol of strength and endurance. In fact, they can live two hundred years or more. It will take more than just a passing wind to blow down a one hundred and five-foot tree. On the other hand, you can pull their roots up from the ground with ease when they're young, but it's going to take some enormous equipment to pull roots up after they've been in the ground for several years; after they're deep and wide.

Similarly, a child who is going to grow up strong in the Lord, and in the power of His might, will not be easy to cut down once they've been rooted and grounded in the Word of God. Once a relationship with the Lord has been built and they have all of His promises written in their heart it will not be easy to tear them down or uproot their faith and trust in God. They'll be planted like a tree by the rivers of water, and not easily moved.

Unfortunately, for me, and many others, our roots were snatched out of the soil before they could get nurtured and woven into good ground. By now I'm about five or six years old. I'm tremendously afraid of my father. Just to look at him had me shaking in my boots. His eyes were empty; when I looked at him I didn't see anybody looking back at me. There was no connection, no spirit to spirit, no bond between parent and child. No glimpse of love. I thought he was mean, unloving, uncaring and cold. I was so afraid of what he would do to me. My concept of him was a man who didn't like me. Actually, I thought there was something about me he hated. His silence was as devastating as his roar. He would go for weeks and never utter one word to me outside of the remarks he made during the whipping for bed-wetting. You know those words, "Why…Don't….You…. Stop….Peeing…..In…..The…..Bed….You…..Ain't….Nothing….. But…..A…..Peeeeee…..Pot!"

Outside of my older sister, I don't think he spoke to the rest of the children either. It's funny how you can talk to each child from the same home, the same parents, and they all have a different story. I'm not sure how they'll write their story but this is how I saw it.

Every time he left the house I hoped he'd never return. When I got much older I realized my father was just where he was. I never knew what his childhood was like. Apparently something happened somewhere down the line in his life to make him act the way he did towards his own children.

Nonetheless, as I grew older my perception about him changed. I forgave him and longed to commune with him. He died at the age of 54; a heart attack, from the onset of Diabetes. I was never able to speak to him as a father; never got to know him as a man. I choose to believe he didn't know any better. Had he known any better I believe he would have acted and reacted differently. I can understand why Jesus said, "Father forgive them for they don't know what they're doing." I would love to have been able to hold a father to daughter conversation with him; he left with so many unanswered questions.

The spirit of fear thought it had uprooted me for good. Yet, according to the Word of God, "For there is hope of a tree, if it be cut down, that it will sprout again, and that the tender branch thereof will not cease" (Job 14:7). In other words, even if a tree has been uprooted, meaning you or I, the love of God which surpasses all human understanding can and will water you with the Holy Spirit and you will sprout again.

The spirit of fear thought it had scared me straight into the arms of the world. I was looking, searching, and digging for love in all the wrong places. For a while it had me, like Joseph I was in the pit of life. Pits don't feel good; people forget about you in the pit, and if you're not careful you can lose hope there.

However, like an archaeologist, I started looking for something I knew I would find. I didn't quite know what it was but I knew it was there and I knew when I found it I would have found a treasure the whole world could appreciate.

I feel like I've been on a long journey. I don't quite remember when it started but it has been and still is the trip of a lifetime. All I know is one day God stepped in and showed me what a father was supposed to be like. It took me a while to open up because of the fear, but eventually I was scared straight into his arms. He delivered me with His love, took away the fear and created in me a new creature. Like Gideon, I went from being a coward to being a mighty woman of valor and like Joseph, what the enemy meant for bad God meant it for my good that much people might be saved.

I can't say it enough, what He did for me He'll do for you. He's not a respecter of persons. Let Him deliver you so you can be all He created you to be, sent you here to be, and expects you to be. God is able!

1. Do you feel like you've been scared straight?

   _____

   _____

2. Has anybody ever tried to scare you into behaving appropriately?

   _____

   _____

3. Do you believe God can deliver you from the spirit of fear?

   _____

   _____

4. What scriptures can help you ward off fear?

   _____

   _____

CHAPTER 3

IT'S A SCARECROW

"Everywhere men and women are confronted by fears
that often appear in strange disguises and a variety of
wardrobes. Haunted by the possibility of bad health,
we detect in every meaningless symptom an evidence
of disease. Troubled by the fact that days and years
pass so quickly, we dose ourselves with drugs
which promise eternal youth. If we are physically
vigorous, we become so concerned by the
prospect that our personalities may collapse
that we develop an inferiority complex and
stumble through life with a feeling of
insecurity, a lack of self-confidence, and
a sense of impending failure. A fear of
what life may bring encourages some
persons to wander aimlessly along
the frittering road of excessive
drink and sexual promiscuity.
Almost without being aware of
the change, many people have
permitted fear to transform
the sunrise of love and
peace into a sunset of
inner depression."

(Martin Luther King STL pg. 115)

M uch of the intimidation the spirit of fear perpetuates is a fictitiously created scene, forming a frightening picture in our minds. These scenes appear to be so real they look like they're equipped with the best of Hollywood's cinematography.

I recall about the age of eight years old staring out my third-floor-bedroom window looking at a branch from the giant oak tree in our front yard. We had moved from a four-suite apartment building that had dirt where grass should have been, to a beautiful two family home with a yard full of grass. My mother believed in moving upwards. She had a desire to see her children grow up in a good neighborhood, one where they could get an excellent education and see a brighter side of life. My family lived downstairs and my aunt's family lived upstairs. Like the Jefferson's we were moving on up.

The first time I saw the house I was excited about the tree in the yard as well as the grass. The tree looked beautiful in the front yard. My four brothers and sisters along with my two cousins and I ran around it, touching it and picking up the acorns, throwing them at each other.

I would finally have my own room and bed. My two sisters, my cousin and I all had bedrooms on the third floor. It had three rooms, two larger ones on each side and one small one in the front of the house that faced the big oak tree on the street. My older sister and older cousin had one window in each of their rooms; they had the bigger rooms. My younger sister and I had two small windows in our room facing the front of the house.

The third floor was stiflingly hot in the summer and cold in the winter. It was so hot and humid in the summer I could hardly breathe. I would sleep butt naked trying to get air from anywhere. Sometimes, to no avail, we would stick our heads out the window breathing in as hard as we could in an attempt to keep from suffocating. It was dark and congested. We each had our own bed, however, I always pulled my little sister over to sleep with me, giving me a sense of security, being that I was so afraid. Later in life I realized both of us were pulling people close for that same sense of security. It caused us to make unwise decisions based on unfulfilled needs.

I loved that big old tree in the daytime for the shade it provided to my bedroom. It had a branch that hung partially across the window right by my bed. In the day it looked like a regular branch, big, brown and barky. However, at night, like Superman, it changed clothes. The only difference was, superman changed to do good, this tree, like a scarecrow, was dressed to frighten you off. I could have easily named it Dr. Jekyll and Mr. Hyde. The branches were fashioned like the form of a human being. It had a head, long body, and two arms. Of course it really didn't; it was just the shape of the limbs. But because I looked through the eyes of fear this is what I saw.

When you look at things through the eyes of fear, they become an image of what fear has created in your mind, a false illusion as to what's real and what's not. The wind can somehow begin to sound like a voice crying out in the darkness, your own shadow starts looking like someone creeping up on you; a tree branch blowing up against the house begins to sound like an intruder pounding at the door; and old creaking floors sound like somebody's creeping up on you.

Many Psychiatrists will tell you it's paranoia, schizophrenia, or a type of phobia. They won't address it as a spirit of fear. Their explanation/diagnosis will not extend into the spirit realm. They will keep it on the natural, physical, biological level. There is a chance you'll find yourself on medication, obtaining counseling and searching for some type of natural remedy. What the church used to cast out, they'll try to counsel out.

Although some people do need counseling as well as medication, chemical imbalances as well as genetic factors often play a part in the problems individuals face. I believe in medical doctors as well as group, individual and family therapy. I've seen it work a multitude of times. Counseling can be highly effective and does have its place. However, when you're talking about the actual "spirit of fear" God warns us about, medication and the like will only be a temporary fix. You'll find yourself going from pill to pill, counselor to counselor wondering why you cannot break free. The spirit of fear does not care about that. It understands one thing; the power of God that delivers and sets men free. Then and only then will we be "free indeed."

In that bedroom fear of the night was overwhelmingly intense and exceptionally frightening due to the darkness. I would purposely keep my eyes away from the window because of the way the branch looked. Unfortunately, somehow my older sister found out I was scared of the tree branch, it probably seemed absolutely silly to her. She looked at it and didn't see what I saw, but she knew I was afraid of it; so being a big sister and wanting to have fun, she took advantage of a perfect moment. She didn't understand the spirit of fear was operating in the midst of us, and she didn't appear to be a fearful person. She was bold, loud, and seemed to be unafraid of anything; at least that's how it looked to me.

One night the wind was howling; threatening, chilling to my soul, it was pouring rain and the branch was steadily tapping at the window. Tap, tap, tap, taunting me at every brush against the glass. I was under the covers scared out of my wits. At this time, she began to shout out how the branch was going to come and get me; how the sound of the wind was the branch making its way in my direction. "Look at it," she said, "It's coming to get you," she shouted out. She went on and on and on. I began to cry and scream out, "stop, stop, stop, I'm scared," but she didn't. The louder and harder I cried, the more she spoke fear into my soul. When it was all said and done, she was happy she had scared me sinless and I was more terrified than ever. My heart was beating like a drum in an African tribe sending out a war cry. We laugh at it now but back then nothing was funny about the tree that had hands for branches.

Nowadays I laugh so hard at some of my terrifying moments. It all seems so trivial now. When I look back at it, that tree was nothing but a scarecrow. The spirit of fear dressed it up in my mind and made me see the image it had created. I didn't see the truth, I saw a lie.

Decades later the spirit of fear is still doing the same thing. At almost four years old, my grandson was struggling with potty training. He had cried, screamed and kicked all the way to the toilet. My daughter and her husband had tried everything with him. He watched Sesame Street, Sponge Bob and other stories on toilet training; nothing helped. They purchased a potty watch that started music every thirty minutes. It's designed to make potty time fun, when it goes off it's a reminder that it's time to use the potty. He wore it and thought it was fun until it began to go off, he would either ignore it or get afraid and start crying because he didn't want to use the potty. They had utilized every tool available to them to assist him in ridding himself of the pull ups and putting on "big boy underwear." Yet, nothing helped. One day she sat him down and very lovingly asked him, "Joshua, why don't you want to use the potty, what's wrong? Mommy and daddy have done everything they can to teach you. Aren't you tired of pooping in your pants?" He looked in her eyes and seriously said, "Mommy, I'm scared." She said, "But what are you scared of, Joshua?" He replied, "I'm scared of the toilet, Mommy, it's gonna eat up my booty." For two years he had been crying about using the toilet. Apparently, he was looking at the toilet and visualizing in his mind a big giant booty-eating mouth. I thought about it for a second and remembered seeing a cartoon with a toilet that talked. I laughed so hard when she told me the story, but then I realized the spirit of fear had him tormented. No telling what the flushing noise made him think of. He probably visualized himself being sucked in by his booty, eaten up, devoured and flushed away.

Most people at some time or another have looked at something, quickly saw something scary in it, looked back and realized it wasn't what they thought it was. I've heard it said some folks are scared of their own shadow, literally. I remember jumping at seeing my shadow, quickly realizing it was me and feeling like a fool afterwards. Who wants to admit they have at some point in time been frightened by a figment of their own imagination; least of all their own shadow.

What are you looking at right now in your life that is causing you fear? Is it a job, a person, a relationship, finances, health? Like the tree limb at my window, what has disfigured itself to scare you into submitting to the belief that it's monstrous, when really it's nothing but a scarecrow?

The natural scarecrow is used in fields to discourage the crows from feeding on the crops. The spiritual scarecrow in our lives is used to discourage us from feeding on the Word; the things of God and the power of God. It wants us to be too afraid to believe the promises of God, the supremacy of God, and the blessings of God.

Like the scarecrow in the field, its looks are deceiving. At first it can be quite frightening; however, if you look deeper you'll see the reality of what it really is and what its created to do. As it hangs in the recesses of your mind, it has labels hanging off of it. The labels say, lack, sickness, torment, hinder, can't, not able, too stupid, people will laugh, don't dare...etc. I'm sure you get the gist of it.

If Job had listened to his wife he would have cursed God and died. He would have been so afraid of the upsetting experiences he was having. First his crops were destroyed, then all of his children died, he lost all his money and his health was under attack. I'm sure after the first few disasters he was thinking, "What's next?" He was still a man regardless of his trust in God, he still felt, hurt, agonized and suffered. Nevertheless, he said, "Though he slay me yet will I trust him." (see Job 13) The scarecrow (satan) wanted to scare him into believing God was not for him; not with him. Satan did not want him to feed on the truth. Instead he wanted him to look at him; a scarecrow.

The scarecrow man creates and puts in the field to scare the crows away from the crops are only designed to do just that. It can't come off its sticks and do anything more than it was created to do. If a man doesn't come and remove it, they have to keep hanging there. They're not able to maneuver in any way unless the man who created it decides this is what he wants to do with this straw dressed up to look like a person. They put the scarecrow where they want, when they want and how they want. It's not meant to actually do any harm it's meant to look like it can. The definition of a scarecrow is: that which frightens or is intended to frighten without physical harm.

Likewise, satan can only move with God's permission, otherwise he's stuck on a pole just like that scarecrow. I believe one of the reasons God allows satan to utilize his scare tactics is to show him that not everybody is going to fall for his illusions; Job was a perfect example. Satan tried with all his might to get Job to take his eyes off of God. Yes, the things that happened to him really did happen. Were they frightening? I believe they were. Nevertheless, Job stood his ground. It would have been most frightening had he renounced God. Thank God he didn't.

Although Job didn't know it at the time, it was God who asked satan, "Have you considered my servant Job?" It was God who allowed the thing that Job feared the most to come to pass. *"For the thing which I greatly feared is come upon me, and that which I was afraid of is come unto me"* (Job 3:25). If Job had looked at the scarecrow and not God, he would have made the biggest mistake of his life. When it was all said and done, God restored Job and multiplied it on top of that. "…also the Lord gave Job twice as much as he had before" (Job 42:10). He gave him double for his trouble and blessed him even more "*So the Lord blessed the latter end of Job more than his beginning…*" (Job 42:12)

There was activity going on in the spirit realm that Job had no knowledge of. The battle was between God and satan. What satan tried to do was scare Job away from God. God knew his servant Job, that's why He asked had satan considered Him. God doesn't lose any battles; He knows the end from the beginning. Once I got that revelation it has not been that easy to scare me.

I believe we are strengthened in the midst of frightening circumstances during our lifetime. We go in seeing satan and come out seeing God. Our courage is built up and we become focused on Kingdom principles. We learn how to be Kingdom minded. We've got to think "God."

As Christians we have the power and the authority of God's Kingdom. We are citizens of the Most High God. He has given us rights. In the United States Constitution there are rights to its citizens. We have the right of the pursuit of happiness and so forth. In the Kingdom of God we have rights as well. In God's Kingdom, we don't have to be afraid because if God be for us then who can be against us? He said wherever we go, He's there with us and surely goodness and mercy is following us all the days of our life. We've got to be Kingdom minded, and know what our Kingdom is all about.

We need to know our King; His persona; His character. We learn these things by going through. How would we ever know the true power of being courageous if we've never been afraid? Ask Gideon who claimed to be a coward how it feels for the Lord to turn you into a mighty man of valor. Ask the woman with the issue of blood about the power of healing. Ask the man by the pool of Bethesda what it feels like to have Jesus come tell you to pick up your bed and walk. Ask somebody who's been homeless, lived in lack, suffered, not knowing where their next piece of bread would come from, about Jehovah Jireh the God who will see and provide. Their testimony will be different from the person who has always had provision and doesn't know what it's like to live totally dependent on God.

God wants us to be aware of every scarecrow we come in contact with. In the movie "The Wizard of Oz" there was a scarecrow who wasn't very good at scaring. This scarecrow looked the part; clothes tattered and torn. It even tried to act the part, but it wasn't convincing. It was a joke to the crows in the neighborhood. They laughed and taunted him because they found nothing frightening about it. Actually, he was empty, shallow, looking for a brain.

The clothes didn't fool the crows, they were aware of the falseness of it. They saw it for what it was, a big bag of straw with a hat on. I read somewhere that fear is "False Evidence Appearing Real." It is a master illusionist. It has the ability to look like one thing but in reality it's something else. While walking out of a theatre after watching a great sci-fi movie I heard people say, "The cinematography was excellent; they made it look so real."

We must come to the realization that our spiritual enemy, satan, wants to attack our minds; our way of thinking. He tries to get us to imagine the worst of what we see and think. He makes it look so real. He tries to torment us with fear. The scarecrows of our minds are imaginations that must be cast down. The Bible talks about this in 2 Corinthians 10:3-5 when it tells us, *"For though we walk in the flesh, we do not war after the flesh: For the weapons of our warfare are not carnal, but mighty through God to the pulling down of strongholds; Casting down imaginations, and every high thing that exalteth itself against the knowledge of God, and bringing into captivity every thought to the obedience of Christ."*

He wants to torment us with our thoughts. Our thoughts determine how we see things and how we see things determines how we react to them. That's why Paul said in Philippians 4:8, *"Finally, brethren, whatsoever things are true, whatsoever things are honest, whatsoever things are just, whatsoever things are pure, whatsoever things are lovely, whatsoever things are of good report; if there be any virtue, and if there be any praise, think on these things."* When our thoughts are not lined up with the truth of God's Word, we become entangled in falsehood. When Kingdom minded, you go right to God's Word. He says, fear not because He's with us wherever we go. David said in Psalm 27:1: *"The LORD is my light and my salvation; whom shall I fear? the LORD is the strength of my life; of whom shall I be afraid?"* It was a long road for me to understand this scripture. I had to come to the realization that God truly is the light of my salvation. Who do I need to fear? He is the strength of my life who do I have to be afraid of? His word works and it needs no defending. "Defend the Bible? I would as soon defend a lion! Unchain it and it will defend itself." *(C.H. Spurgeon)*

When we are abnormally afraid, it hinders the move of the Holy Spirit who wants to guide us in all truth. Fear positions itself to appear as though it were reality. When this happens we find ourselves walking in darkness not in the light. As children of the light we don't have to stumble in the darkness. If indeed God is our Shepherd what do we have to be afraid of? The Good Shepherd is the greatest protector of all mankind.

When we are Kingdom minded, we think Kingdom principles. Therefore, when frightful situations occur we revert to the Word. I have learned through all of my struggles that "Because I dwell in the secret place of the Most High I'm abiding under the shadow of the almighty. He is my refuge and my Fortress, My God, in Him will I trust. I know without a shadow of a doubt that he will deliver me from the snare of the fowler. I don't have to be afraid of the terror by night nor the arrow that flies by day" (Psalm 91).

When you are Kingdom minded you think about what's going on in the Kingdom of God not in front of you. I spent many years looking in front of me but glory be to God He showed me beyond my natural eyesight. I got a glimpse into the realm of the Spirit and began to see the power of God.

He is a strong tower, our refuge, the righteous run in and they are safe. (see Proverbs 18) Walking in fear prevents us from walking in faith. God wants us to walk by faith and not by sight. He wants our thoughts to be obedient to His Word.

I was hindered for so long due to the spirit of fear. There is no way God could have his way in my life as long as I was frozen in fear. My thoughts were fearful, I comtemplated the worse, imagined a Boogey Man under every pillow, a ghost in every closet and a monster under every bed. I spent precious time scrambling around scared.

Nevertheless, Romans 8:28 says, *"And we know that all things work together for good to them that love God, to them who are the called according to his purpose."*

Years of suffering have a tendency to draw you closer to the Lord. It assists you in knowing who He is and finding out who you are. If you continue to go through and God continues to bring you out you can't help but know Him to be a deliverer. If you've been sick almost to death and He brings you out, you can't help but know Him as a Healer. If you've been frightened to the core of your bones and he gives you Holy Boldness you can't help but throw your hands up to the God who has not given you the spirit of fear but of power, love and a sound mind and praise His Holy name.

Because I was so afraid it was easy for the scarecrows of life to intimidate me. I remember there was a play at school and my teacher had given me a part. She knew I was extremely introverted. I don't know why she did it. God bless her heart. Maybe she thought it would be therapy for me. It was an unsuccessful attempt to get me involved; to bring me out. She invited all of the parents and made a big thing out of this play. I studied those lines for what seemed like an eternity. Yet, when the time came for me to step up and recite my lines, I froze. I peed in my pants; I was so scared it was devastating. All I saw around me were scarecrows. I felt so ashamed, stupid, not worthy.

The thought of being too afraid to do something you know you can do makes you want to kick yourself in the butt. It makes you want to stick your head down in the sand like an Ostrich, ashamed to show your face. The spirit of fear has a tendency to make you feel "undeserving" of being successful. You walk around guilty of being afraid.

As a teenager in high school I was so afraid of being judged, of measuring up to the other teens that I walked the halls during lunch period to keep from going in the cafeteria. I simply could not face having to deal with their remarks, their inconsiderate ways, their volatile behavior; I was too afraid, cowardly and weak.

There was another girl that walked the halls also. She was a short, chunky Caucasian girl with long stringy straight hair. She and I never spoke to one another, and although we didn't speak, we had an unspoken understanding of what was going on. I thought she was short, fat and ashamed of what she looked like. She probably thought I was another individual like her; scared to death of going into the cafeteria. If I went to a corner to sit down and she was there, I'd keep going. If she came to a place to sit where I was, she'd move on. We did this for quite a while. Actually, it went on until I dropped out of the eleventh grade. I sure would like to know what happened to her. I hope she got delivered like I did. God forbid she's still hiding out somewhere.

When I got older it dawned on me that the teachers didn't appear to be concerned about two troubled young ladies hanging around in the hallway. They never lifted a finger to find out what the problem was. They allowed these two obviously troubled teenagers to walk the halls every single day during lunch period. We knew they saw us; they would walk past oblivious to our predicament. Anybody that's hiding out in the hallway every single day is obviously riddled with issues. It's one of those things that make you go Hmmmmmm. Unlike them, I've got a mandate to get the word out that you don't have to be afraid of the Boogey Man.

Back then we both had some serious scarecrows going on. I'm grateful to God that He does see and He does deliver. The power of His Word and His love is awesome. While the scarecrows of my life were having a field day, the Lord had a purpose and a plan for it all. Little did I know that one day I'd be standing in front of huge crowds, singing to the glory of God, and ministering His Word. In the Kingdom of God, all things are possible.

Get ready because God is going to release a Holy Boldness on you that will make your head spin. He's going to deliver you from the spirit of fear and start moving you toward your destiny. This is the beginning of a brand new day. God is able!

1. Have you had scarecrows in your life?

_____

_____

2. What is dressed up to put you in a state of fear?

_____

_____

3. Do you believe God can open your eyes and reveal the truth?

_____

_____

4. Write down everything you are no longer afraid of.

_____

_____

CHAPTER 4

DEVIL, SHUT UP

And they were astonished at His doctrine: For He
taught them as One Who had authority, and not as the
Scribes. And there was in their Synagogue a man
with an unclean spirit; and He cried out, saying,
Let us alone; what Have we to do with You, thou
Jesus of Nazareth? Are you come to destroy
us? I know You Who You are, the Holy One
Of God. And Jesus rebuked him, saying,
Hold your peace, and come out of him.
And when the unclean spirit had torn
him and cried with a loud voice, he
came out of him. And they were
all amazed insomuch that they
questioned among themselves,
saying, What thing is this?
What new doctrine is
this? For with authority
commands He even the
unclean spirits, and
they do obey
Him.

Mark 1: 22-27

In the Garden of Eden the serpent was talking to Eve; in the wilderness he was tempting Jesus; through Peter he was speaking to Jesus; throughout the Bible he is talking. It appears as though every time he spoke, his motives were egregious. As human beings we have a hard time comprehending anything talking but us, except perhaps a parrot. Yet, according to the Bible the serpent and Eve were holding a conversation. Not long after talking with the serpent the Bible says Adam was telling God he was afraid. One minute they were with God walking in the cool of the day, the next minute they were hiding from Him and afraid. You better know you have a talking enemy.

A spoken word is a powerful thing. God creates with words. He said, *"Let there be light and there was light, let there be a firmament in the midst of the waters, let the waters under the heaven be gathered together unto one place, let the Earth bring forth grass, let us make man in our own image"* (Genesis 1). Powerful and wondrous things happen when God speaks. Words have been and always will be a source of power.

The enemy knows the power of words, so he talks and he talks and he talks. He lies, twists things around, contradicts, accuses, and causes chaos. He is the father of lies. From Genesis to Revelation he has had something to say. He got in trouble by talking. With his narcissistic persona he said, "...*I will ascend into heaven, I will exalt my throne above the stars of God: I will sit also upon the mount of the congregation, in the sides of the north: I will ascend above the heights of the clouds; I will be like the most High* (Isaiah 14:13-14). What possessed his vain, egotistical, self absorbed and conceited self to think for one moment he could be like the Most High God? That alone goes to show you he'll say and do anything that'll promote his agenda, which is to steal, kill and destroy.

I learned through pain and suffering that he repeatedly spoke to me; times when I had no clue. He spoke through friends, family members, co-workers, neighbors, and yes, church folks. He talked when I was a baby, he was talking when I was a toddler, he had a whole lot to say in my teenage years; he kept talking while I was a young adult, continued talking even as I got older; started talking like crazy when I made up my mind to serve God with everything I had in me. Now, before you put this book down and start thinking I'm crazy, hear me out.

As a teenager I was beginning to venture out into who I was. I was curious about a lot of things; exploring, discovering. I was starting to have a little confidence in my ability to communicate with others and I loved to sing. At this time I was dating a young man who could also sing and play the piano. I had a crush on Paul Williams of the Temptations and thought he looked like him. Being that I couldn't have Paul he was the next best thing. We were in my basement listening to music one cold winter day when I decided to take a big leap of faith and sing in front of him. The music had been playing for quite some time. We were enjoying Aretha, the Temptations, Marvin Gaye and one of my all time favorite Gladys Knight and the Pips. The music had infiltrated the fear that previously crippled me. I was feeling like a part of the gifted Motown crew. As I opened my mouth and let the first note flow out he began to frown. "Oh no," I thought, "You are not going to ruin my opening night." I shut my eyes and kept on singing. I remember the song, it was Aretha Franklin's "Until You Come Back To Me." Nobody could have told me I wasn't getting down. I loved that song from the first day I heard it, I loved anything Aretha sang. She wasn't just the Queen of Soul, she was soul. She could sing Mary Had a Little Lamb and I would get excited. I continued singing, "Until you come back to me that's what I'm gonna do, I'm gonna rap on your door tap on your window pane open up baby, I'm gonna rap on your door, tap on it tap on it tap on your window pane." Oooooh it sounded good to me! When I finished singing I opened my eyes to see the biggest snarl looking back at me. I said, "Well." He said, "You sounded so doggone country." I couldn't believe he was saying that, it was like a sharp dagger in my heart. I stared at him, speechless, not knowing whether to hit him or cry. He didn't stop there, then he said, "Whoever told you you could sing?" By this time my mouth was wide open. He got up, walked out and left. Almost as though he was outdone by the mere audacity that I thought I could sing. I was crushed; didn't sing for quite a while either. I didn't want to chance that happening again. People will chew you up, spit you out, and not even suffer with indigestion. After that he no longer looked like Paul of the Temptations either. He started looking like the grim reaper.

Singing for me wasn't something I just did, it was who I was. One Christmas, at about the age of eight, my mother purchased a radio with a record player attached. This was the best gift I'd ever received in my whole life. Apparently, she knew I loved music and thought it would be something I would enjoy. Christmas was great at our house, you would think my mother spent her life out. She made sure we had everything and then some.

Because I was severely shy and introverted, not even to mention the fear, I would spend quite a bit of time off in the corner somewhere listening to music. It was my way of being involved without being involved. I would pretend I was singing with whoever was on the radio. I sang with some of the greatest artists: the Supremes, Smoky Robinson, the Temptations, Aretha; Oh, and I loved Otis Redding, the Wright Brothers, Dean Martin, Tony Bennett; I simply loved music. I knew all the songs and all the words, the background, who wrote it and what recording company they were with. I could hide in music, it would take me away to melodic heaven where I fit; where my soul could be at peace. It was a world within a world; a place where fear could not reside. So when he made a mockery of my singing I was disheartened and dismayed to say the least, and yes, now that I look back, I think the spirit of the serpent was talking. Ok and maybe I didn't sound that good either, but still.

If you believe the Word of God, then you believe the serpent was talking in the Garden of Eden. He slid right up next to Eve in a subtle way questioning her about what God did or didn't say. Did you know the spirit of fear talks as well? Yes, it does. It actually has a conversation with you. It speaks words of doubt and despair. The problem is you often speak back in agreement.

If you're a writer fear may come straight out and say, "You can't write, nobody's going to buy a book written by you, who wants to hear from you anyway." You in turn listen, don't write the book and start agreeing with the spirit of fear by saying to yourself, "I can't write a book, nobody's going to buy a book from me, who wants to hear what I have to say anyway, what do I know." Or it might question you in a subtle way by asking, "Are you sure you can write? Have you ever taken writing lessons? Remember you didn't do too well in English (He's good at reminding you what you didn't do well at). Do you think you're called to do something else?" You hear the questions and begin doubting your abilities. Talking to yourself you say, "Well I've never taken writing lessons and it would be better if I had a degree in English." This is also true with the song you didn't sing, the poem you didn't write, the picture you didn't paint, the audition you missed on purpose, the game you never played, the college you never attended, the business you didn't start, and so forth. Those daunting questions about who you are or your capability to create can hinder the purpose and the plan for your life; they hindered mine. Your potential becomes stagnated and perhaps even aborted by words spoken by the spirit of fear.

When I look around and see great things accomplished by mere people, I wonder how they did it and if they were afraid. I've come to the conclusion that some people were afraid and some were not. It doesn't matter who was or who wasn't. What does matter is if they were afraid, they did it anyhow.

If Michelangelo had succumbed to fear, the world wouldn't have The Last Judgment in Rome at the Sistine Chapel or the statue of David. Without Leonardo da Vinci we wouldn't have the Mona Lisa or The Last Supper. Without George Frideric Handel we wouldn't have Handel's Messiah. Martin Luther King Jr., admitted in his writings, of the fear he dealt with, rose above it and changed America in such a profound way. Mahatma Gandhi's courage was tested at a time after being slapped, kicked and pelted with stone eggs he stated, "God has always come to my rescue...my courage was put to the severest test on 13th January, 1897, when ....I went ashore and faced the howling crowd determined on lynching me. I was surrounded by thousands of them...but my courage did not fail me. I really cannot say how the courage came to me. But it did. God is great" (Gandhi The Man, His People, and The Empire p. 81). This great man admitted to almost losing courage in the face of adversity.

He said he didn't know where it came from, yet, he ended his statement with "God is great." He knew God was great enough to pull him through one of his toughest times. At that time they had been shouting out, "Thrash him, Thrash him." Sounds almost like crucify Him doesn't it?

All of these men had something in common. They went forth regardless of the opposition they faced. Apparently, they rose against whatever could have hindered them. They painted, sculptured, sang, wrote, created, marched and defied. Whatever they needed to do nothing but death came between them and their purpose. If they could tell you about the voices designed to stop them the conversation would probably be a lengthy one; endless. They took the wings God gave them and flew above the turbulence designed to keep them down. Like an eagle they rose above the very wind intended to break their flight. They took lemons and made lemonade. Moreover, the same God that brought them to their destiny can take us to ours. Hallelujah for the Lord God Almighty Reigns!

Martin Luther King Jr. knew the hounding voice of fear, he had experienced it far too often. Ghandi admitted to being tested with his courage. When the devil shouts at you those words can sound like a howling demon straight from the wickedness of hell. He knows what to say. He has a way of getting under your skin, harassing you, planting seeds that'll help his plan come to fruition, not God's plan. God wants to prosper you, fear wants to destroy you. God wants to lift you up, fear wants to bring you down.

God said His sheep know His voice (John 10). If His sheep know His voice then what other voices are we hearing, and why would He need to tell us this? It means there are other voices masquerading as light. The voice may be your own or the voice can be the voice of tormenting and hindering spirits. They speak the opposite of whatever God is saying. They're tricky, conniving, sneaky and deceitful; subtle.

Once again we've got to be Kingdom minded. Otherwise, we'll succumb to the voice bent on destroying us. Years will roll by before we realize who we've been listening to. When you have a relationship with God you are familiar with His voice. Although I wasn't as close with my father as I would like to have been, no other man could fool me by imitating his voice. I knew that sound too well. Even so, the world is full of great imitators. Men get paid huge amounts of money for imitating others. But God cannot be imitated. His voice is unique, divine, loving, sharp, and totally perfect. How can you imitate that, it's impossible.

Before I had a relationship with the Lord, and knew His voice, I was easily tricked. Fear had me and it had me good. I know what it's like to be so afraid your body aches with pain and your soul cries out to hide in the nearest darkest corner. I know what it's like to be ridiculed in front of people who laugh at you in your face, who scare you with their insidious remarks, snares of hate and voices of doubt. I know what it's like to want to soar like an eagle but instead you walk around balking like a chicken. I know what it's like to hear the voice of the enemy yelling in your ear gates, "Give up now, who do you think you are; nobody's going to listen to you. You can't do that. You are not equipped, you don't have the credentials, you are a has-been, and your time is up. You waited too long. It's too soon. Your past is too horrendous. God hasn't chosen you for this." I know what it's like to listen to his voice one moment and listen to God's the next. No, it's not easy. You want to give up. Your spirit man says listen to God, but that voice keeps talking. I've been there. Sometime there is only one thing to do and that is to shout out from the top of your lungs, "DEVIL, SHUT UP!!!!" Somebody said, "It's not polite to say shut up." Who's trying to be polite to the enemy of their soul? You think he cares about courtesy?

That voice spoke to me for so long I had to struggle to hear the voice of the Lord. It was like being a slave and only knowing the command of an evil master. I had to drown out negativity, shouting, murmuring, complaining and cursing. In my lifetime I had heard little encouraging, so I didn't know what it sounded like. I hadn't heard love talk; didn't know the sound of it. This made it hard to hear the voice of a sweet and loving God. I never heard I could, so this gave the enemy the door to come in and say I couldn't. Whatever it was I tried to do I heard, "You can't." This didn't come from a living person, it was a spirit speaking; one that wanted me to be afraid of the world, of me, of any chances to grow, to come out from wherever I was in that hiding place and thrive.

I'll never forget the first time I sang in front of a crowd. Yes, I kept on singing regardless of whether it was country or not. The gift of song was embedded in me and I couldn't help myself. I was at a neighborhood bar, sitting at a back table alone, watching the people and listening to the music. I loved to go in there and watch the musicians play and hear the singers. I was fascinated by their courage to stand in front of all of those people and exercise their gift. The keyboardist would be hitting those keys like he was made for them, smiling, enjoying the moment, while the drummer and guitar player followed with such ease. This was one of those times I'd peep out and see the wonderful things going on wanting to be a part of it.

On this particular night their regular lead singer didn't show up and they asked if anybody in the audience could sing. As I slowly lifted my hand I could hear the spirit of fear saying, "Did you forget you sound country?" I should have said, "Get thee behind me satan." However, to be honest with you I wanted to immediately back down, but the guitar player who saw my hand up in the crowd was already calling me to the front. Everybody's eyes immediately shifted toward me as he gestured with his hand. My heart was pounding inside of me. I remember thinking, "What the hell am I doing. I'm getting ready to make the biggest fool out of myself."

I cannot believe I remember the song. It was Natalie Cole's "Peaceful Living." I grabbed the microphone like I knew what I was doing. I'm talking about a girl who was still afraid of her shadow. Nobody can tell me God isn't able. I told them what song to play, looked around at the musicians, kind of gave a little nod and waited on them to begin to play. While I was listening for my cue to begin singing I noticed I couldn't see the faces of the people. I didn't have my eye glasses on because I hated wearing them; being called a four-eyed fool so often in school was not an incentive to put them on; I chose temporary blindness instead. Furthermore, glasses were so doggone ugly back then. Now here I stand, blind as can be, and for the first time in my life I'm glad I can't see.

Every time I read the first chapter of Jeremiah where God tells him not to look at the faces of the people, I get tickled. I know from first-hand experience the benefit of not looking at their faces. Their faces tell lies. Some of them are yawning, some smiling, others are snarling or looking away; can't look at their faces. God told Jeremiah I've got a plan for you and nobody's face can detour what I have already set in place.

Don't look for approval from the faces of men for you may never get it. Their faces change like the wind. It may blow in your direction one minute and blow in another direction the next. For the faces of men are never consistent. Their approval is often temporary and their love wavers depending on the moment. God's face is the only face that doesn't change. His love is everlasting even until the end of time. Only when you look into the face of God will you see the pure truth.

I began to sing looking out at a complete blur. I stumbled for the first second or so, then I sang as if I were in the room all alone, nothing but the orchestra and me. I was that little girl in the corner singing with everybody on the radio. They were playing it in the perfect key. At this very moment the enemy of my soul did not exist, I could no longer hear any remarks. The voice had been hushed, and I flowed in the spirit of who I was in the gift of song that God had given me, I was in heaven. For the first time in my life I was doing it afraid. If I said I was not scared I would be lying. The truth is, I was, but I didn't care. People in that audience had no clue they were experiencing "the miracle of the night." When the song was over they all began to clap, people stood up on their feet and were yelling, "sing again sing again." I could feel tears swelling up in my eyes, I was overwhelmed; utterly surprised. Finally, I had a break-through. I read somewhere that a breakthrough is an advanced case of knowledge. I knew at that moment if I didn't focus on the faces of the people, I would be better off, and it was their faces I feared the most. If anybody snarled I never knew, if anybody yawned I didn't see it, if anybody walked out I could have cared less. All I knew was, I was in heaven. The Spirit of God was all over me and I was free as a bird.

Over the years I've kept that same attitude. You can't afford to look at the faces of people. Don't bother with trying to make sure they approve. In addition, don't spend time worrying about what they're thinking. As long as you are following the Spirit of God, and you believe in Him and what He has in store for you, all is well.

I left there that night a new person. I still had an awfully long way to go but oh what a beginning. I was smiling and laughing with people, my head wasn't down and I felt like somebody worth something. In the twinkling of an eye God had lifted me up. He did it in a neighborhood bar around people who were drinking, smoking and doing God knows what. The Lord is like that, He does what He pleases and nobody, absolutely no one can question His will for another. We get religious and begin to talk about how, where, and what God would and wouldn't do for His people. That's why I try not to be quick to judge anybody. We don't know what people have been through. We have no clue what's going on in their hearts and minds. We don't know how the Lord will deliver them, but we know He will.

When the Scribes and Pharisees saw Jesus eat with publicans and sinners, they couldn't understand it, they wanted to know what He was doing. They couldn't comprehend how He could be so anointed, so powerful and be seen eating with a sinner. They simply could not grasp that concept.

Jesus was eating with them then, and He's eating with them now. I thank God He's Omnipresent because He was sure in that little neighborhood bar with me. He showed up and placed me right in front. He knew what I had been through and what would help bring me out. That night he spoke and he spoke loud. He shut the devil up good. Oh How I love Jesus!

Jesus was notorious for operating out of the box. He went and got fisherman to disciple instead of going in the synagogues, He ate with tax collectors who were in line with the Roman oppressors, He made the best wine and then he turned around and kicked over tables. They didn't know what Jesus was going to do next. He kept them scrambling around trying to figure Him out.

In Jesus' time whomever you ate with meant you were linked with them, sharing your reputation so to speak. The religious leaders considered this behavior to be wrong; in their eyes, Jesus was acting disreputable. They couldn't understand how He could eat with low life and still cast out devils. They couldn't stand the anointing that was destroying yokes and removing burdens. They wanted Him to be more like them, hard, harsh, and unloving. They wanted Him to be kicking butts on their behalf. It sounds like they were listening to the wrong voice. For if they were hearing the voice of the Lord, they would have heard, *"And lo a Voice from Heaven, saying, This is my beloved Son in Whom I'm well pleased"* (Matthew 3:17). If God is well pleased, who are we to complain? Have your way God.

Sadly, they didn't hear the Voice from Heaven. They heard a voice telling them not to heal on the Sabbath Day even if it meant leaving a man with a withered hand. They were unloving; unkind. The Bible says this after Jesus healed the man's withered hand: *"And the Pharisees went forth, and straightway took counsel with the Herodians against Him, how they might destroy Him"* (Mark 3:6).

Why? What voice was they listening to that would make them want to kill Jesus for healing a man's withered hand on the Sabbath?

The Herodians were a group who believed that Herod was the Messiah, and the Pharisees normally hated them. Isn't it funny how your enemies line up together as soon as they have a common cause; hating you. People that couldn't stand each other all of a sudden find something to talk about; you. You can tell when your enemy has gotten help, all of them decide they're best buddies and you are the outcast. Remember, wolves run in packs.

I want you to ask yourself this question. If God didn't have a problem with Jesus, remember He said He was well pleased, and Jesus didn't have a problem with healing on the Sabbath Day, and He was God wrapped in flesh; then whose voice were they listening to? Who actually had a problem?

I submit to you my brothers and sisters, it was that same old serpent type spirit still talking. One day, and it's coming soon, that voice will be hushed, shut up, thrown into the lake of fire never to be heard of again. Hallelujah!

Jesus had authority over demon spirits; and if He didn't want them talking they didn't.

And there was in their Synagogue a man with an unclean spirit; and he cried out, Saying, Let us alone; what have we to do with You, Thou Jesus of Nazareth? Are you come to destroy us? I know you Who you are the Holy One of God.

And Jesus rebuked him, saying, Hold your peace, and come out of him (Mark 1:23-25).

In other words Jesus was saying shut up and come out. We are not conversing, there is nothing to say, just get out. That spirit came out; immediately.

This is a perfect example for us. I'm not talking either; shut up and get out is my motto. Your words of fear have no power here, they have been annihilated, dispelled, castrated by the powerful Words of God. Your mission has been aborted! Hold your peace. In the name of Jesus!

There is another instance in the Bible when Jesus had to chastise satan. When Jesus started telling His disciples about the suffering He was getting ready to go through and how he would be killed and raised in three days, Peter took and began to rebuke Him saying this is not going to happen. Jesus turned to Peter and said, *"Get thee behind me satan: you are an offence unto Me…"* (Matthew 16:23). Satan hadn't done anything physical. You didn't see him, the only person standing there was Peter. Peter was the one talking. This tells us that satan talks through people. That's why we have to be careful who we allow to speak into our lives. You can't have everybody and anybody having something to say about what's going on in your life. Some people may be sincere but they can be sincerely wrong. They could very well be speaking from the voice of satan. You've got to know when a "Get thee behind me satan" moment arises.

Don't listen to every doctrine that comes blowing with an evil wind. People will talk you out of the biggest blessing you've ever had.

In this season of my life I've learned to prophesy over myself and I encourage you to do the same thing. When I wake up in the morning I start decreeing and declaring words over my own destiny. I get up and say out loud, "This is a great day. I am prosperous this day. I am fulfilling the purpose and the plan God has for me daily. Absolutely nothing is going to hinder my walk. Mountains shall be leaped over; obstacles shall be overcome by the power of God. Resurrection power down in the bowels of my very being shall be utilized to the glory of God. Arise, shine; for my Light has come, and the Glory of the Lord has risen upon me." I wake up the next week continuing with the power of words by saying, "God's doing incredible things. This week He's going to make the impossible possible, the unreachable reachable and the unbeatable beatable. He's giving me strength to stand against the invincible and I thank God that His Kingdom is unshakable. His leadership is comparable to none. His guidance is perfect. This week He's taking me to a higher place in Him; drawing me nearer and I'm excited about going. God is able!" When I sleep and then wake up because He has sustained me, my feet hit the floor and I start saying, "Lord, I thank you for this day. May it be filled with your Glory. God, I pray that when the sun goes down and the moon begins to rise I would have met my expected end for these twenty-four hours you have so graciously blessed me with. If for some reason Lord I haven't met my expected end, forgive me O God, and I thank you that your mercy is new every morning; therefore, tomorrow I have another opportunity to meet my expected end again. How Great Thou Art." I think about the enemy and his tactics and I say to myself, "Wait a minute, I am walking in full authority. My mouth is like a scud missile. When I let out praise it goes forth and begins to execute vengeance on my enemy. In the matchless name of Jesus I can ask anything according to His will and He will do it. I am so full of the Holy Spirit I can speak light into every dark situation I face and darkness will be dispelled. My Father has placed His Word in my mouth and has commanded me not to be afraid." At that moment I let out a praise from down in my belly that the enemy, though he may try, cannot control. My God and His Word are faithful.

If you believe God and His Word, then you know there are some things He will and won't say. You learn His voice by spending time with Him, worshipping, praising, reading His Word, meditating on it, asking questions, and being in His presence. He said, *"Call unto me and I will answer you and show you great and mighty things that you did not know"* (Jer. 33:3). He wants His sheep to hear His voice. Let Him minister to your soul as He reveals Himself to you like never before. When God talks the enemy shuts up.

1. Do you believe the spirit of fear talks?

   _____

   _____

2. If so, did it speak to you?

   _____

   _____

3. Do you believe you can talk back?

   _____

   _____

4. Start telling fear to shut up when it talks.

   _____

   _____

CHAPTER 5

WE SAW THE GIANTS

And Caleb stilled the people before Moses, and said, Let
us go up at once, and possess it; for we are well able to
overcome it. But the men that went up with him said,
We be not able to go up against the people; for they
are stronger than we. And they brought up an
evil report of the land which they had searched
unto the children of Israel, saying, The land,
through which we have gone to search it,
is a land that eateth up the inhabitants
thereof; and all the people that we
saw in it are men of a great stature.
And there we saw the giants,
the sons of Anak, which
come of the giants: and we
were in our own sight as
grasshoppers, and so
we were in
their sight.

Numbers 13: 30-33

Typically, when we think about a giant we visualize something or someone extraordinarily tall with big feet, huge hands, a large head and towering over us. Even the word "giant" sounds overwhelming. It's defined as something unusually large, being of great stature and strength. A giant is often thought of as bigger than life. They are not always big people; many things can be considered giants; an illness, an academic test, a troubled relationship, an unhealthy body, unemployment, even in our attempt to lose weight we find ourselves facing what appears to be an unbeatable giant.

God spoke to Moses telling him to send men to spy out the land of Canaan. He was giving this land to the children of Israel. He was to send from each tribe of their fathers a man, everyone a leader from among them; twelve all together. Unfortunately, the Bible says ten of the men came back saying, "We are not able to go up against the people, for they are stronger than we." They said it was a land that devours its inhabitants, and all the people they saw were men of great stature. The giants were so big that the men looked like grasshoppers to the giants and to themselves. They were afraid of their immense size and strength, the sheer thought of having to fight them was agonizing. Only two men thought they could overcome the giants, Joshua and Caleb. They believed God and were ready to press forward. Unfortunately, I didn't have a Caleb nor Joshua type testimony. Like some of you, there have been times in my life when I could relate to the ten men who came back with an unfavorable report; the ones who were afraid.

My first day at Jr. High School was riddled with giants. I was a twelve-year-old girl transitioning to unknown territory. My anxiety level was at an all time high and for the first time I wouldn't be walking to school with either of my brothers or sisters. One of them was attending the local High School, two were still at the elementary school and one was with me. However, we didn't walk together, I walked alone. Looking back at it, if I was him I wouldn't have walked with me either. A few weeks before school started I began to suffer with what I believe now to have been a vaginal yeast infection. I had scratched my skin raw due to the unbearable itching. Consequently, I walked with my legs wide open in a desperate attempt to keep my raw skin from touching. It was the most uncomfortable feeling, and the most embarrassing, traumatic, event a girl of twelve years old could face. My brother probably said to himself there is no way I'm going to walk to school with her. I most likely looked totally ridiculous and shamefully awkward; I was in absolute misery. My skin was hurting, itching, burning; I couldn't think due to the frustration and embarrassment of this dreadful situation. My mind was spin-ning around and around and I wanted to literally disappear. I was already nervous and frightful about attending a new school, the last thing I needed was to draw attention to myself. My God, my soul looks back and wonders how in the heck did I get over? Thank God He is able!

The halls of this new school appeared to be long, spacious; never ending. They had an echo like an old abandoned castle. I remember trying to find my first class. As I walked down the hall with my legs strangely shuffling, attempting to maintain the slightest comfort I could, a couple of boys looked at me and laughed, I could have melted in the floor. If I had stretched my arms out I would have looked like Frankenstein. I painfully wanted to dart off into the nearest hiding place. But I continued, scared, worried, anxious and self-conscious. I'm sure I looked physically challenged. I thought everybody must be looking at me. I wondered will I ever make it to the end of the day; my life is over. Throughout the day searching for each classroom was like looking for a needle in a haystack. I was lost physically, spiritually, mentally and emotionally. It was as though I was in the "Twilight Zone."

It had to be the spirit of the Living God that helped me make it through the first day of class. On my way home, I cried like a baby. I did not want to go back to school, not under those conditions. The giants were going to devour me. I wasn't like Caleb. I was not well able to overcome, no how, no way. I was like one of the men who looked at the situation and said, "Look those giants are too big and there is no way we're going to conquer them, it is absolutely impossible!" I looked like a grasshopper to them and I looked like more of a grasshopper to myself.

Some of the children were nice but some of them were mean as all hell. I was timid, shy, broken, ashamed, ridiculed but most of all I was terribly afraid. I already operated out of the spirit of fear, now it had been magnified. Like the ten men I saw the giants, I didn't see God and I surely didn't see anything in me. The only thing I was able to do was run like Forest Gump "Run, Darlene, Run, Darlene, Run." I could have gone to the Olympics with my tracking ability; it felt like I could do a 500 meter run in a matter of seconds. I was not ashamed to run from the giants.

When people know you're afraid they tend to take advantage of your weakness. That's why I believe God tells us over and over in His Word to fear not. He knows the enemy will take advantage of our fears. He'll hone in on your fears and rip into your very soul with negative words and horrendous images. He'll magnify the problem and make you forget you have a problem solver (Jesus). He'll make a molehill look like a mountain. He'll do it so subtly you won't know what hit you. He'll have you afraid of something that never was, all the while, keeping you from the blessing of something that surely is.

I cannot imagine the fear children have to face today in schools riddled with drugs, guns, rape and even murder. I am sure they are afraid when they awake daily to face giants most of us never knew existed. These giants eat up all of their inhabitants. We never know what day we'll turn the news on and hear of another school massacre. They never know what day they'll walk in that building never to walk out. Without a machine-gun, how are they able to overcome this monstrous giant bent on killing whomever it chooses? I know it appears to be getting worse but I do entertain hope that one day we'll rise to the occasion; put prayer back in school and protect our children with the power of God. In the meantime they're machine-gun is the powerful Word of God.

Not only are our children facing giants, adults have to deal with them on a daily basis. We fight them at work, in our homes, our communities, our jobs, our relationships, the government and in our own minds. We have to gear up daily as if we're going to fight in Baghdad.

Make no mistake, in life we will face giants. They come in all shapes, sizes and forms. However, just because they're giants doesn't mean we are grasshoppers. We are well able to overcome, not because of us, but because of the spirit of God that lives in us.

I'm not saying everybody should be happy-go-lucky and never be afraid of anything or anybody. People in the Darfur region of Sudan have a reason to be afraid. Millions of them are hungry and millions have been displaced by violence. The killings, rapes and volatile environment they've had to live in since the war began is heartbreaking. I cannot fathom having to wake up every morning not knowing whether a gang of cut throat savages are going to kill me, my family or our neighbors; a giant walking towards me with a hatchet in his hand. The strongest of mankind will feel the agonizing pain of fear while living under such atrocities. These fears are founded on basic human instincts. I believe Samson himself would have trembled when faced with the brutality of innocence these people are faced with consistently. They have a legitimate reason to be unbearably afraid.

Being afraid because of what lies ahead when dealing with murder and mayhem is understandable. We should all have a healthy fear of what's going on in Darfur. There but for the grace of God go I. The whole world somehow revolves around itself. Either we will face judgment for standing by and doing nothing, or else one day not so far in the near future, an atrocity like this will find itself to our shores. This is a fear we should be addressing today not tomorrow.

However, this fear does not compare to the unnatural fear of a child looking at a tree and seeing a monster. It doesn't compare to a grown man not wanting to come out of his house from fear of people he's never seen. This is a different giant; one that is embedded in your psyche. This is a spiritual giant that must be fought with much prayer.

How do you learn how to fight giants? One way you learn how to fight them is through adversity. I was watching my grandson and his friends play a video game one day. They were having the greatest time fighting with what looked to be a superhero battling his enemy. They finished one section and before they could go into the next this is what appeared on the screen *"SPAR WITH YOUR TOUGHEST RIVAL IN ORDER TO IMPROVE YOUR SKILLS."* I Jumped up and said, "That's it, that's it. I believe God allows our rivals to toughen us up; to sharpen our skills!"

God wanted the Israelites to improve their skills so he opened the door for them to spar with their toughest rival: the giants. The great thing about God is the rival may look tough to us, but He is well able to overcome even our toughest enemy. God is a God of possibilities. *"And Jesus looking upon them saith, with men it is impossible, but not with God: for with God all things are possible"* (Mark 10:27).

The giants I faced then, and continue to face even now, have only served to strengthen my faith. Like many of you, I have sparred with giants of self esteem, physical, emotional, and spiritual; you name it, and I've sparred with it. I've fought some giants that appeared to be unbeatable. Yet I fought like a crazy lady. I was fighting so hard somebody had to tell me I had won. In it all, I was taught how to see God and not the giant. I had to stop looking at myself saying I can't and begin to look at God and say He can. I realized God is able to do the impossible. I got the revelation that He could take my natural, put some super on it and allow me to do the supernatural. How awesome He is. God is great and greatly to be praised! Oooooh Wheeee! Once I found out the power and the authority of God, the giants begin to look like Gods' tool for me to spar with. My toughest rival was only improving my skills.

Ten spies looked at the people. People can be intimidating when we look at their faces, status, abilities, and gifts, they look like giants. The problem is not in the people, it's in us and how we compare ourselves to them. The book of Corinthians says they measure themselves by themselves and measure themselves with themselves, and that is not wise. It does look insurmountable when we observe what others have to offer, begin to compare and decide we don't measure up to them.

On the other hand, when our focus is on what God has placed within us, our outlook becomes more promising. I like Mariah Carey's song "Hero" because it encourages you to know there's a hero within. I call it the "Spirit of God" that dwells within me. I believe we were all born with "hero" status down on the inside of us. We spend too much time looking for a hero and when our hero lets us down we get angry, depressed, and feel betrayed. The problem is all people are subject to error, no matter who they are, no matter how anointed they are, or what the call is on their life. Moses, David, Abraham, Jacob, Peter, Paul all erred. Yet, God used each one mightily and David was a man after God's own heart.

Should our public figures be responsible? Sure they should. However, we need to keep in mind that they are people with problems and issues. We don't need people to stand tall for us. Our God has equipped us with the ability to stand taller than any giant if we only dig deep within, get our eyes off of "people" and on Him. Know that our hero lies within.

There was a young lady whom I counseled several years ago. She had been molested by two family members and abused by another. When she looked at other young women, she compared herself to them in a negative way. She saw herself as damaged goods but looked at them as pure, whole vessels. She kept herself isolated because of the shame she felt in the company of people who she thought was better than her. She was always afraid they'd find out the terrible secret of her past. She would have panic attacks when the subject of rape, molestation or child abuse came up. In their faces she saw judgment, rejection and disgust. There was one lady in particular that made her feel the worse. This young lady was pretty, educated, articulate, drove a nice car and had an outgoing personality. By looking at her you would think she was an all-American, perfect female, having had a wonderful life. But what you couldn't see is what she had actually been through. She had been raped by her father since the age of ten. Her mother, who knew about it, did nothing. She was ostracized from her family for finally exposing her father's crime to a school social worker, who informed the authorities and had him arrested. He's currently incarcerated and will be there for years to come.

I invited both of them out to lunch hoping somehow her story would come out. When the young lady who looked like she hadn't been through anything began to share her story, the troubled young lady's mouth flew open and did not shut for several minutes. She told her I never would have known you went through this. She replied, "I was victimized almost half of my life. I refuse to allow that spirit to keep me in bondage. My father and my mother should be ashamed not me. I have forgiven them and moved on. I have this one life and I am going to enjoy it." She looked in her eyes, held her hand and said I advise you to do the same thing.

Perception, however real we may think it is, can be deceptive. Giants can, and often do, look much bigger than they really are.

Looking at the giant will stop you from going into your promised land. It almost prevented me; I was on the verge of giving up because I kept looking at the giants. What's my promised land? It's to be in a place of fulfillment, utilizing my existence for the purpose and the plan as ordained by my creator. I believe when he looks at us and says "Well done my good and faithful servant" that he's saying I did well what he sent me here to do. I remained faithful to His call. Has it been easy? No, it has been one of the hardest things I've ever had to do. It's easier to look at the giants, give up, walk away, back down, back out and be done with it. It's easier to come up with excuses as to why I can't. I could be like Otis Redding sang "Sitting by the dock of the bay watching the tide roll away." I could continue to be like one of the ten spies and say, "I look like a grasshopper to myself and I look like one to the giants too," or I can be like Caleb and say, "Come on let's go. We are more than able to overcome."

It looks like either God's missed it or we've missed it when we look and see giants in the land. We begin to question ourselves as well as God, asking questions such as; How can I do this when I have a giant standing in the way of my finances? Where am I going to get the resources? Oh, I love this one...They won't let me? I'm still trying to figure out who "they" are.

Think about the following questions: Would Martin Luther King Jr. have ever received the Nobel Peace Prize for his work to end racial segregation and discrimination had he seen the giants of hatred and bigotry and ran in retreat? Would Mahatma Gandhi have pioneered satyagraha—resistance to tyranny through mass civil disobedience which led India to independence and inspired movements for civil rights and freedom across the world, if he had seen the giants of discrimination and oppression to a people and allowed them to stop him? Would Barack Obama be the first African American President of the United States of America if he saw the giants of a system designed to systematically conquer and divide, using among other things, racism, and allowed it to stop him? Obviously, the answer is no. These men saw the giant but they boldly chartered through unknown territory and made their way to their promised land. I believe God sent each one of them to do exactly what they did and are doing. The giants they faced were enormous, lives were lost, but they faced those giants and beat them. You might ask, "If they beat them why did some of them die so horrifically?" Martin and Mahatma both died but they also live through the sacrifice they made for others. They beat the giants by fulfilling the purpose as to why each one of them was born. Jesus died on the cross but yet He reigns. I'd rather die for something of a noble godly cause than live for nothing or run away in fear all my life.

Ludwig van Beethoven continued to compose, conduct and perform even after he was completely deaf; the giant that disabled him from hearing his own music had no power over his destiny. The giants of blindness and deafness didn't hinder Helen Keller, though it may have tried, from being the first deaf/blind person to earn a Bachelors Degree of Art. God is a miracle worker indeed.

How can we live up to our potential without fighting a giant or two? Getting past the giant will get you to the next level; new level, new devil, so they say. I heard someone say no adversity equals no opportunity. Sometimes you've got to do it afraid.

It is not the critic who counts: not the man who points out how the strong man stumbles or where the doer of deeds could have done better. The credit belongs to the man who is actually in the arena, whose face is marred by dust and sweat and blood, who strives valiantly, who errs and comes up short again and again, because there is no effort or shortcoming, but who know the great enthusiasms, the great devotions, who spends himself for a worthy cause; who, at the worst, if he fails, at least he fails while daring greatly, so that his place will never be with those cold and timid souls who knew neither victory nor defeat. (Theodore Roosevelt)

In other words President Roosevelt was saying: Don't just sit there, get up and do something. Nothing beats a failure but a try. If you fall on your face you did better than the guy that did nothing. If you get up when you fall you're doing better than the guy that falls and lays there.

A young lady was complaining about problems by stating, "There is always something; why can't I live with no problems?" I told her as long as there is always something that means you "are." The day there is nothing, that will be the day that you "aren't." Life entails many obstacles and these barriers force us to reach deep down within our very being and exercise the power that lies within. Otherwise, we would never have the opportunity to know exactly how strong we actually are. It wasn't until I sparred with my toughest enemy that I realized how strong I was. Before then I sounded like Gideon. I thought my family was the least and I was the least of them. Fortunately, God showed up, told me who I really was and moved on my behalf. He opened my eyes an allowed me to see through the spirit.

The first thing is to see the giant. Then through faith and prayer come up with a plan to bring it down. As we look at the giants, and they will be there, let's remember we have a God that's bigger than they are. Let us first trust and believe if He sent us to it, He will bring us through it. Let's hold on to the promises of God despite the giants that appear to be standing in our way; determined within ourselves that there's no giant big enough to withstand the power of God. I like the fact that He is in complete control. If He could take the world and hang it on nothing like He said in the book of Job, then without a shadow of a doubt He can strengthen me to fight a giant or two. OK, maybe we have to fight three or four; giants appear to be coming from out of nowhere nowadays.

Think about it, in the land God promised the Israelites the fruit was so big it took two men to carry one cluster of grapes. Because the giants were the inhabitants of that land they were obviously the ones tilling it. They were not tilling it for themselves, although they probably thought they were, because the Lord had given that land to the Israelites. He was using the giants to prepare the land for them. I believe because the land was so rich and great, God placed giants there to prepare it for His people. This way when the day came and his chosen people arrived they only needed to walk in and take of the land flowing with milk, honey, full of pomegranates and figs just as God had promised.

What made the ten men say they saw themselves looking like grasshoppers and the giants saw them looking like grasshoppers? Nowhere in that scripture does it say the giants thought they looked like grasshoppers. Are they trying to say they heard the giants say, "Look at them they look like grasshoppers?" They didn't hear the giants say anything. They heard their own minds speaking. They thought they were small and because of this they thought the giants were thinking the same thing. "For as he thinks in his heart so is he..." (Proverbs 23:7). The way a man thinks determines how he perceives, and how he perceives, determines how he proceeds. I've heard people say they were afraid because of what "the people" thought. Many times the people never told them what they were thinking. The person simply thought people were thinking negative of them because they were thinking negative of themselves.

I wondered why they would choose a grasshopper to compare themselves to. Perhaps they saw themselves looking like grasshoppers because snakes eat grasshoppers. Maybe they immediately visualized the serpent (snake) whipping out his tongue; devouring them with his venomous bite. Doesn't that sound like the spirit of fear to you? When faced with what looks like a "giant problem" we see ourselves small, create a scenario of defeat in our minds and run for cover like a grasshopper.

The grasshopper has big hind legs for hopping. They are perceptive and can sense you when you are several feet away. When they think they're in danger they begin to hop. When we see what we perceive to be a giant we start hopping. We hop to sex, dope, lying, depression, food, shopping....I'm sure I can go on and on. If we weren't a grasshopper to begin with, we become one by the state of our mind. They thought it, then they said it, then they told it to others, who believed it. They created a domino effect of faithlessness that cost the Israelites forty years in the wilderness, when they were right around the corner from their promised land. They let the fear of giants define who they were. Never allow men and circumstances to define who you are or what you can do. Always keep your head up knowing that you were created for a specific purpose.

Be like Caleb and Joshua; know that you are well able to overcome. You might be at the brink of a breakthrough. Your promise land may be right around the corner. Don't be that close and see the giant. Be that close and see God. God is able!

1. Are you dealing with some giants in your life now?

_____

_____

2. Do you see a big giant or a bigger God?

_____

_____

3. Are you like the ten spies or like Caleb and Joshua?

_____

_____

4. When faced with a giant what will you see?

_____

_____

CHAPTER 6

I WILL FEAR NO EVIL

The LORD is my light and my salvation; whom shall I
fear? The LORD is the strength of my life; of whom
shall I be afraid? When the wicked, even mine enemies
and my foes, came upon me to eat up my flesh, they
stumbled and fell. Though an host should encamp
against me, my heart shall not fear: though war
should rise against me, in this will I be confident.
One thing have I desired of the LORD, that will
I seek after; that I may dwell in the house of
the LORD all the days of my life, to behold
the beauty of the LORD, and to enquire
in his temple. For in the time of trouble
he shall hide me in his pavilion: in the
secret of his tabernacle shall he hide
me; he shall set me up upon a rock.
And now shall mine head be lifted
up above mine enemies round
about me: therefore will I offer
in his tabernacle sacrifices of
joy; I will sing, yea, I will
sing praises unto
the LORD.

(Psalm 27:1-6)

Currently, the world is in a state of chaos. Things are looking more frightening by the hour. Every time you turn on the news there is murder, wars, sickness, anger, division and racism; somebody's hurt, somebody's crying and somebody is dead. I've never seen so many entire families being murdered at one time: husbands, wives and children. Even the church is no safe haven. The enemy is marching into our sanctuaries in broad daylight killing men and women of God. Hatred is at an all-time high and respect for another life appears to have been flushed down the drain. People are ready to kill at the drop of a hat. Our public officials are disrespectful and think nothing of it and parents curse the teachers out right after the child does. Even the weather appears to be out of control. Storms such as Katrina and tsunami's are leaving people dead and homeless by the thousands. Volcano's that have been dormant for some time are erupting and causing uproars.

Where are we as a culture; a society; a world? How did we get here and more importantly how do we get out? Mankind is in a scary place right now. When men make decisions based on fear and cannot reason together because of it, that's a dangerous place to be. The enemy doesn't have to touch us; all he has to do is deposit the spirit of fear and walk away. We'll take care of the rest on our own, as we are doing. Who is listening to the voice of reason, the voice of love, compassion and truth?

Right now I believe the spirit of fear has been unleashed throughout the world. It's designed to divide us, to make us see one another as the enemy. Democrats are afraid of the Republicans and the Republicans are afraid of the Democrats. Countries fear other countries will annihilate them with nuclear weapons so they prepare to defend themselves. Fear has everybody protecting themselves from everybody else. We're all guarding our lives for fear of the invader. Because of what we see in the natural, I can understand why we're afraid. Yet, because I believe in the power of God, I'm praying that those who believe His Word will fast and pray for our eyes to be open.

When I look at what's going on now I think about how the Lord delivered me from fear; this strengthens my faith to know He can do it for the world. He is a holistic God; body, soul and spirit as well as person, country and universe.

I've been through many things, some warranted fear but many didn't.

Out of all the things I've been through one of them really stands out. In the early ninety's I went to the Dr. for a routine checkup. I was told I had a hard knot in my colon. The surgeon performed a biopsy which came back malignant; I had colon cancer. When the Dr. informed me I had cancer, he basically told me to prepare myself for death, to go home and get my house in order. The surgeon asked, "Do you have any children?" "Yes," I replied, with a quiver in my voice. He said, "Oh I'm so sorry," as he looked at me with the most pitiful look he could conjure up. The first thing I thought of was my daughters, my nephew, my son, and my mother. I cried out, "Oh Lord I don't want to leave my children and what about my mother."

My sister had a history of drug abuse and was about to lose custody of her children. I knew I was going to have to raise my nephew who I love as my own son. I didn't want him to have to go to anybody else and I knew my sickness would jeopardize that; he had been through more than enough already. I secretly cried for my son, because at that time we still had no knowledge of his whereabouts and only me and my oldest daughter talked about him or looked for him. I always had a fear I'd die never having met him. The fear was more for him than for me. His father had already passed away years before; my passing would leave him void of ever meeting either of his parents.

I had a child at the age of seventeen and another one at eighteen. Their father was in a mental institution during the second birth. Unfortunately, I put him up for adoption because I feared not being able to provide him with sufficient care. At that time having babies out of wedlock was not as prevalent as it is now. I was considered a deviant which contributed to lower self esteem and fears I already suffered with. Although I don't agree with children born out of wed-lock I understand it. I was searching for love and peace, not knowing it was within me. It was not the sexual act that drew me; it was the contact love from another human being. I needed to be touched, comforted and verbally esteemed. A father's love would have elimi-nated an endless search for something only a father could give. How many other women can say the same thing?

We can't judge with an iron heart and not take into consideration the reason why out of wedlock births are prevalent in our society. Where are the fathers? Where are the responsible adults? Where is the love? Why are we sitting by and simply doing nothing but railing accusations and blaming?

Here I was a teenager, uneducated having dropped out of the eleventh grade, no husband and two kids. On top of all that I was still full of the spirit of fear. My poor oldest daughter, while she was growing up we had this big closet in our apartment, and I used to make a pallet in there for us to sleep on because I was afraid of the dark. She thought we were having fun. I would say, with as much excitement as I could muster up, "Come on let's get in our secret hiding place, bring your toys and I'll bring my stuff." She thought it was the greatest thing. I would pretend as though we were camping out. We had a light in the closet with one of those long pull strings. I took books, food and her toys in there for what she thought was a night of enjoyment. We wouldn't come out until daylight hit. The thought of this child having to endure growing up this way can only shed light on how faithful God really is. He kept her and protected her in spite of being raised by a mother who was clearly ill equipped to handle motherhood.

It would have been wonderful to have kept my son. Although I could barely take care of the child I had, somehow I think we could have made it, closet and all. We searched for him for over thirty years. Thank God for the Internet. We found him through an online people-search service. God showed my oldest daughter exactly which site to go to. One night we were talking about him and I told her I needed help finding him. That very same night she called me back. I'll never forget the moment she said, "Ma I think I've found him." I said, "Oh my God, I hope it's him." She begin to tell me how there was a young man on this site, looking for his family, with the same birth-date and born in Cleveland. At that very moment I knew it was him. Who else could have been born that day, in that city, and looking for us? We started investigating every lead we could find until one day we hit the mark and found him. Since then we have met him, his children and his adoptive family. They are all wonderful people. In spite of my inadequacy God has blessed him with loving parents and has protected him. When I look at him and his children I am reminded of fears ability to lead a person into making decisions that are contrary to what their heart truly feels. Fortunately, God's mercy is able to surpass man's shortcomings, and although I'm reminded of a bad decision, His grace reminds me of His love. He can make the worst thing the best thing. God is able!

After the Dr. gave me the bad news I thought this is not a good time, God, I can't die now. Don't you want me to raise my baby? Don't you want me to be here for my children? Don't you want me to live Lord? Don't allow my mother to lose another child; it'll kill her. Please Lord spare my family from the agony of loss and defeat. Who's going to comb my daughter's hair (her hair was so long and thick, it touched the top of her behind) we used to call her Cousin It from the Adams family, because she was so tiny with all this hair covering her little frame. I asked God who's going to call my mother every day, five times a day, who's going to make sure my oldest daughter doesn't slip off into a depression that'll take her out of here? Who's going to make sure my nephew gets a hot meal every day, somebody to esteem him, and a permanent home?

I was actually reasoning with God. In 11 Kings 20, the Lord sent the prophet Isaiah to tell Hezekiah to set his house in order because he was getting ready to die. The Bible says he turned his face to the wall and asked the Lord to remember how he had walked before Him in truth and with a perfect heart and did good that which was in God's sight. God heard his prayer and sent the prophet back to tell him He'd give him fifteen more years to live.

I didn't know I could reason with God. I prayed out of a sincere heart and desperation. I couldn't pray like Hezekiah did, I couldn't say Lord remember how I'd done anything. All I could say was remember my daughters; why should they be left without a mother, remember my mother why should she lose another child?

And remember yourself didn't you send me here to complete your purpose and your plan? Why let the devil take me out ahead of time? Giving God something to think about can't hurt. I took it back to Him. Life begins with Him and ends with Him.

The bottom line is I was afraid, had no control over my situation. I couldn't heal myself and none of the people I loved could heal me, not my family nor my friends. I learned at that moment how dependent I was on God. I called on Him and prayed for mercy. I needed him to reach down into the bowels of hell and bring me out. I had never known this kind of fear, it was different. It wasn't a scary fear but a fear of reverence unto an awesome God. I was awestruck about His power over life or death. I was afraid of whether He would honor my prayers, my requests, and my desires.

My oldest sister, who has always been my Joshua, came immediately when she found out, she prayed to God like He was right in the room; because He was. Afterward, my family went with me to the first Oncologist meeting, asked questions and supported me as I went through the biggest trial of my life.

While I was under the care of the Oncologist, the pain and suffering was almost too much to bear. As I went through the chemotherapy and radiation, my body was oftentimes wrecked with pain. The agony drove me closer and closer to God. Every time I urinated my body would go through convulsions, because the area they radiated was next to my bladder. I would pray, Lord, I know you're watching and I know you'll bring me out. I believe you see what's going on and you will have compassion on your ailing daughter. I prayed, when I saw my weight going down; I prayed, every time I saw the worried look on my daughters' faces.

While the spirit of infirmity appeared to be destroying my body my oldest daughter couldn't take it, so she tried to commit suicide. I'd leave the radiation session and go visit her at the hospital where they had her in the psche ward; I was still praying. The child that grew up with me, sat in the closet with me, watched me go through hell from the time she was born, needed my prayers regardless of my situation; and I prayed. My youngest one would sit in the bathroom on the floor as I went back and forth for hours from the tub to the toilet. She stayed there keeping me company, holding onto her mother as my body convulsed. She watched me shake and writher while death pounded at my door relentlessly; and I prayed.

It was as though I was suspended between life and death. The spirit of death was pulling me one way while the spirit of life was pulling me the other way. It was an intense power struggle, one that lasted for months.

Death tried to destroy and annihilate me before my time. Nevertheless, I was determined to stay here, I knew without a shadow of a doubt I had things to do, people to support and a God that wanted me to fulfill a plan and purpose. But it was hard, honestly it was. Death kept knocking; it was trying its best to send me into a tumultuous state of fear. I struggled and wrestled with it, back and forth, fighting like a baby in a lion's den. Fear was shouting,

"Give up, you can't handle this, it's too much, back down and back out." Only this time, I wasn't listening. I said, "Devil, shut up. You may have frightened me all my life, but no more. I have had enough of you. You tortured me when I was a toddler, scared the living daylights out of me as a youth, humiliated me as a teen, and held me back as an adult. You may have been a strong foe for me, but you're not stronger than my God. He's bigger than you, greater, and on top of that you've got to answer to Him." Oooooh Wheeeee! Oh How I Love Jesus!

Through this trial I learned how to fight like a gladiator, using the sword of the Spirit, and the shield of faith. I obtained skills beyond human comprehension while sparring with my greatest opponents; death and fear.

I kept calling on the name of the Lord, my healer, my deliverer. He is the only one who could answer a cry without sound, a heart cry, the cry of a soul hopeless without the intervention of a mighty God. I called on Him like a baby crying for its milk at the mercy of a woman's breast. The hunger for His love and protection had become deeply ingrained within my soul. Thank God, El Shaddai, the many breasted one was and is all sufficient. As I cried, He began to give me a vision of who I was, and for the first time in my life, I could see God had a plan for me. He took me all the way back as a little girl and showed me how He stayed with me even when I thought I was alone. He showed me how He helped me in math class when I thought I was incapable of completing the simplest mathematical problems. He gave me a sweet encouraging teacher who was patient and kind. It lifted me up so high that years later I would be in college obtaining a degree in accounting. He strengthened me as a teenager when I was looking for love in all the wrong places and showed me all I needed was Him. He kept me from hurt, harm, and danger when I took myself places where if it had not been for the Lord, I would not have come out. I've never had a venereal disease, even though I did not use wisdom in the 70's, in regards to sexual relationships. He showed me how He kept my mind sane while I was trying out dope and alcohol. God has a sense of humor. When I tried out marijuana, I thought I was going to die with a heart attack. I remember my heart pumping and feeling like it was about to explode. It boggled my mind as to why anybody would want to smoke it. When I tried to snort cocaine, I didn't feel a thing and thought it was a waste of time so I never tried it again. When I was about fifteen years old, I tried taking acid; I itched all over my body so bad I wouldn't dare try that again. I'm telling you I have definitely not been an angel. I was looking and searching for something to give me peace, a sense of belonging, a sense of joy, just to find out it didn't exist in all those things. God showed me how vengeance was His and how He'd take care of my adversaries if I would only put my trust in Him. He showed me Jehovah Jireh and how He had been the father I needed when my baby and I were sleeping on the floor in an apartment all alone on the verge of getting evicted. He showed me how He provided me with transportation, money and food when we were in desperate need. He took me, a young lady with no high school diploma, through a couple of Associate Degrees, a Bachelors degree and a Masters Degree. He took me from a shaking, straight-up scaredy cat to singing thousands of miles away in London; not only at one church but ministering at several. He taught me how to stand strong, not backing down, but to boldly walk by His Spirit. He gave me courage to stand in the midst of adversity knowing He was right there with me. Every time I started to give up I'd hear Him whisper softly in my ear, "I'm right here with you, go ahead, move forward." He has never let me down and I'm sure He never will. He can do everything but fail.

Had it not been for the mercy and grace of God on my life I would be a crack addict, an alcoholic, a strawberry, a thief, a liar, cheat, sneak, freak; everything the enemy of my soul wanted me to be. This is the reason why I can't afford to be judgmental, there but for the grace of God go I. My goodness, How Great Thou Art!

I learned throughout this process that God will make a way out of what looks like no way. That He has everything in control even when it looks totally chaotic, like the state of the world right now. Everywhere I go, I encourage my brothers and sisters by saying, "Know this my friend, every mess is an opportunity for a message. Every test is a chance to testify to the goodness of God. Every trial is an opportunity for a triumphant outcome. Every tear is an opportunity for the hand of God to gently wipe His glory across your face. Every ounce of pain is God's opportunity to deliver you, and every time you call His name, it's an opportunity for Him to answer, and show you great and mighty things that you did not know." God is Able!

While going through this adversity, it felt as though I had a case against me for committing a crime and if I was convicted I would be sentenced to death. I visualize a courtroom with me as the defendant, the devil as the prosecutor, Jesus as my attorney and God as the judge. The devil is accusing me of being guilty of many things and deserving death. Jesus comes forth and reminds the judge that although I had committed a crime the price had been paid. The enemy rants and raves every accusation he can think of; exaggerating and lying. However, the judge won't hear of it. No matter what accusations the prosecutor hurled at me mercy and grace said "No." Finally, when the judge has had enough he hits the gavel hard and says, "Case dismissed."

Had I never been through the pain and suffering I endured I would have never known the power of God. Had I never needed God to provide for me I would have never been able to say like David, "The Lord is my shepherd I shall not want" Had I never had the spirit of infirmity all over me, I would have never been able to speak with confidence and authority that He is the Lord God that healeth thee.

I can only thank Him for allowing me to suffer with Christ because I can truly say, "Now I know." I don't think it, I haven't read about it, I haven't just heard about it, I know all about it from my own personal experience. Because of the spirit of the living God, I will fear no evil. He is too big, too great, beyond comparison and more than capable of keeping me.

There is nothing, nobody, no situation nor circumstance that can hinder the move of God. If He called you to it He will see you through it. Ask David; ask Abraham, Moses, Joshua, Rahab, Joseph, Jacob, Job, Gideon, Ruth, Deborah the Prophetess, Peter or Paul, even Isaiah whose time God extended.

God equipped each one of us before the foundation of the world was formed to complete a particular task. Everything you will ever need is already inside of you. He is able to do exceedingly and abundantly above all you can ever ask or think. If you're thinking it He can do better than that. He has the answer to all of your questions before you utter them out of your mouth.

Once I was delivered from the spirit of fear, I felt like a lion that's been in captivity all its life, and is finally free and able to roar. Oh what a relief it is to be as free as a bird. That's why I long to see people free from the bondage of fear. I can understand why Harriet Tubman went back to help slaves obtain freedom, even risking her own life to do it. She had experienced something that she couldn't keep to herself. She wanted others to feel the exhilaration of knowing you can fly if only given a chance.

Operating in fear is a form of slavery. For most of us imagining someone enslaved to another is unfeasible. We don't see people being led off in shackles nor do we see them being auctioned off like cattle. As a result we cannot comprehend being enslaved to some-thing or someone. For the most part, we feel as though we are free. Yet, the spirit of fear has enslaved us in ways that no man can. I've heard it said by many prisoners you may lock me up physically but you'll never lock up my mind. Fear does the exact opposite, your body will be free but your mind will be bound, ball and chains.

Until I knew I was struggling with the spirit of fear, I thought I was just scared. There is a difference. By the time I was an adult, I had made crucial decisions based on fear. These decisions shook the very foundation of who I was. I gave my child up for adoption, afraid I wasn't capable of providing for him. I fell into relationships for fear I couldn't be left alone. I backed out of open doors afraid to go in for fear I'd be rejected. I held back on talents and gifts the Lord blessed me with because I didn't see myself the way He did. Fear had me like an African slave born and bred in the midst of slavery. To be born as a slave inhibits you from knowing the true meaning of being free to be you. Yet, within your soul is a free man dying to experience the freedom you were created to behold, that freedom that's raging in your inner man. Thank God, whom the Lord sets free is free indeed.

Like a slave owner; the spirit of fear uses its power in diverse ways. Slave owners allowed some slaves to work in the house and some in the field. The slaves in the house had it considerably better than those in the field. So goes the spirit of fear. Some people are functional: they hold down jobs, raise their families and even run businesses. While others suffer with fear that leaves them taking pills, seeing psychiatrists, counselors, running hither and thither for a cure, and spending all they have like the woman with the issue of blood. All the same, they are all slaves. The business owners keep their foot on the necks of the workers for fear they'll rise up and move beyond them. Those holding jobs are fearful of the employer one day handing them a pink slip, so they shuffle around scared to do the least thing wrong, even going to work deathly ill for fear of being fired. Oh yes, there is fear in so many unseen ways.

The Lord doesn't want us to be slaves to fear or anything else. He created us to be free; to soar like eagles. Look around and see the freedom of God's creation. I am astounded by the sun, the moon and the stars. When I see an airplane flying I'm amazed at how man could create such a thing, I was laying back on my bed with my hands behind my head snuggled up against a downs pillow looking out my window to the heavens, amazed at the awesomeness of God. As I looked beyond what I see with my natural eyes envisioning what lies afar, how can I be afraid of the little I can see when there is so much more that I don't see? When I feel the wind blow against my face, I'm experiencing the matchless act of God. Who else can control the wind and the direction in which it blows? Who else can take the world and hang it on nothing and it doesn't fall off into oblivion? Who else can keep us from falling off the earth as it rotates around the sun at about 67,000 miles per hour? As I laid there looking at the awesomeness of God I realized, this God, this creator, is my Shepherd and I have nothing, absolutely nothing, to be afraid of.

I've learned its ok not to be afraid of the unknown. Looking out into the vast universe of God's creation what is there to be afraid of? Every morning when the sun rises, it's obvious He's in control. At the sunset of every evening He is still in control and in the midnight hour when I gaze upon the stars, each one standing at attention, having a name given to them by God, obedient to its creative call, I am in awe of who He is. Psalm 147 says he knows each star and has named them. He heals the broken in heart and binds up their wounds. This alone takes away the fear of not knowing, the fear of tomorrow, and the fear of uncertainty. How can I continue to fret over things I have no control over? Why should I be afraid to shine like the stars or rise like the sun when I too am created by the God of all. I will fear no evil.

We should not be struggling with who we are. Nothing God created seems to struggle with what it is but man. You will never find the sun struggling to be bright, nor will you find it wrestling to get to the sunrise or the sunset. In its obedience unto the Lord it rises and sets at its scheduled time; no fight and no resistance. You won't find the moon opposing its appointed place in the dark of night nor will you find the stars struggling to shine as they lay across the sky looking like white lights lying against black satin, being held not by gravity but by the very hand of God. If fear were to hold the sun back, humanity would freeze to its death, and if it moved any closer out of fear, man would be obliterated by the heat of its substance. The existence of mankind depends on the obedience of God's creation. If this is so, then how much more does the existence of mankind depend on the obedience of His children? As far as I know, for us, there is one sun, one moon, and each star is uniquely designed to shine with its own light. There is one you and one me—we don't have to be afraid of what the next individual has in comparison to another. You and I are a designer's original. We were specifically created by a masterful potter with a purpose in mind. Just like the sun we must rise to the occasion and like the moon let us brighten up the darkness of this world. We may look like we have crevasses and our light may appear dim at times. There are times we're at half moon because the issues of life prevent us from shining at full force, but shine anyhow realizing a half moon is only for a season; keep waiting you'll see its fullness in due time. Fear not when life seems dim and your light appears to have diminished. The sun may go down but keep waiting the sun will come out tomorrow. God is still commanding "let there be light." God is able!

When I was a little girl I feared death, I used to cry, "I don't want to die." I thought I would never live past my twenties. Seeing myself as an older woman was not a part of my vision. The spirit of fear had me so shaken that longevity was not something I thought would ever occur. However, after much adversity and years of suffering through troubles and sickness, maturity set in and a change occurred. Now as an adult, the only thing that matters is God's plan. My attitude changed to, "I want to live to fulfill the purpose and the plan for my life, to max it out and enjoy every moment of it." I believe the same

God that took care of me will take care of my children. Therefore, the enemy can't scare me with death. *"O death, where is your sting? O grave, where is your victory?"* (1 Cor. 15:55) David said, *"Yea, though I walk through the valley of the shadow of death, I will fear no evil: for you are with me; Your rod and your staff they comfort me"* (Psalm 23:4). Once you've been through the valley of death, you recognize it as a shadow because God has taken the sting of death away. He learned he didn't have to fear death. Through all David faced, he found out one thing for sure and that was he didn't have to fear. Fear had tried to torment him over and over. He said in Psalm 3, *"Lord how are they increased that trouble me. Many are they that rise up against me, many there be which say of my soul there is no help for him in God; but thou, O Lord, are a shield for me."* He learned that no matter how the enemy came up against him he was still under the protection of an almighty God full of mercy and grace. In Psalm 23 he said, *"Surely goodness and mercy shall follow me all the days of my life."* You know why he said that, because every time he got into something, goodness and mercy got him out.

We have to fight fear with faith in God, utilizing the Word of God. When Jesus was tempted in the wilderness He fought back with the Word; got to have the word in your heart and be prepared to utilize it at any given moment. Jesus was not afraid and His trial was the harshest of them all. He walked, talked and moved through the spirit with authority. Fear has no place in God. It's like a foreign object in the body that gets vomited out. When Jesus died it looked like it was over but we all know it wasn't. Although you have feared many things and it appears as though you have gone down, fear not, God is going to rise you up. The same way Jesus rose, we too will rise, and one day He's coming back. Hallelujah, and until then, I am not afraid of the Boogey Man, therefore, I will fear no evil. How about you?

1. What do you now know about the spirit of fear?

   _____

   _____

2. Are you still dealing with unnatural fear?

   _____

   _____

3. Do you know God has not given you fear?

   _____

   _____

4. Will you continue to fight fear to fulfill the purpose and plan for your life?

   _____

   _____

One thing I know about God is this: He is able. He was able when He created the Heavens and the Earth. He was able when He saved Moses in the basket. He was able when He saved Daniel in the lion's den, able to keep the Hebrew boys safe from fire and smoke. Able to create a mighty man of valor out of a confessed coward, able to heal a woman who had an issue for twelve years, able to make whole another woman who had been bent over for eighteen years. He was able to deliver a young frightened little girl like me from the spirit of fear. He was able to send His son to redeem a world he loved, who died then rose and is now sitting at His right hand. The same God who was able then is able now. God is able! – Darlene Wade